DEEP ENOUGH FOR IVORYBILLS

Deep Enough for Ivorybills

by James Kilgo

with illustrations by the author

Anchor Books

Doubleday

New York London
Toronto Sydney Auckland

AN ANCHOR BOOK
PUBLISHED BY DOUBLEDAY
a division of Bantam Doubleday Dell Publishing Group, Inc.
666 Fifth Avenue, New York, New York 10103

ANCHOR BOOKS, DOUBLEDAY, and the portrayal of an anchor
are trademarks of Doubleday, a division of Bantam Doubleday Dell
Publishing Group, Inc.

Library of Congress Cataloging-in-Publication Data
Kilgo, James, 1941-
        Deep enough for ivorybills.
        1. Hunting—South Carolina. 2. Fishing
—South Carolina. 3. Nature. I. Title.
[SK125.K55   1989]   799.29757   88-28298
ISBN   0-385-26014-8 (pbk.)

Deep Enough for Ivorybills was originally published in hardcover by Algonquin
Books of Chapel Hill in association with Taylor Publishing Company. "Deep
Enough for Ivorybills" was first published in *The Sewanee Review* and "Actual
Field Conditions" was first published in *The Georgia Review.*

for Jane

Contents

Author's Note

A PROPER SONGFEAST HAS three parts. The first is the event itself, the experience which provides occasion for the singing. My experience has been rich because of the people I have walked with and the paths we have traveled. Like all experience though, it has also been at times both random and ephemeral. In the desire to make sense of it and in some way to keep it, I have tried to sing about it, to tell what happened. That is the book—the second thing. The third is the giving of gifts. Since, alas, I don't have enough meat and furs to go around, I can only offer instead a full measure of gratitude . . . to all with whom I have shared a cup of coffee or a warming drink on a cold and windy day; each of them is present here, especially Milton Hopkins, Rick Belser, Grainger McKoy, Bob Benson, Lee Tebo, Jim Meunier, Clark Ivey, and Jeff Carter; to Rob Winthrop and the members of the T. Huntington Abbot Rod and Gun Club, especially Hilburn Hillestad, Ken Ware, Jerry Varnado and the late Don Terry; each of the fourteen others, too numerous to call by name, knows his place at the long pine table; to the three John Kilgos—father, brother, and son— who got me started and have kept me going; and to four special ladies—my mother Caroline, my wife Jane, and my daughters Sarah and Ann, who in that order have endured my comings and goings, my odd hours, muddy boots, and scattered gear.

Those have been there and know better than anyone else whether or not I have held a true note.

And also to these: Joe Bailey, whose call from Alabama one night was the real beginning of this book; each member of the little writers' group that came together at the right time and lasted just long enough; Coleman Barks, poet and friend, who taught me the words; Paul Zimmer, Phil Williams, Mike Nicholson, Judith Cofer, Betsy Cox, and Judson Mitcham, who encouraged me; Stanley Lindberg and Mary Hood, whose faith in the book I could not have done without; Louis Rubin, whose sound judgment made it better; and Marty Carter, who gave up her time and her dining room table for two months to an impatient writer and a word processer.

Athens, Georgia   JAMES KILGO
January 10, 1987

DEEP ENOUGH FOR IVORYBILLS

1
Deep Enough for Ivorybills

WE USED TO CROSS THE Big Pee Dee River on our way to the beach each summer. The steep drop into the floodplain always surprised me. For two breathless seconds at sixty miles an hour we seemed to hang on the crest of the hill, high above a wide green floor, reposed in the sun below us. "There it is," my father would say, "the Pee Dee River Swamp. You get lost in there, they'd never find you." Even as he spoke, we would go hurtling down and then, at the bottom, level out onto the long causeway that shot straight across the swamp like a yardstick.

A gloomy wall of forest crowded the road on either side, but when you hit the bridge you could look for a long way up and down the wide, sunny reaches of the river. Here and there a cypress tree, streaming Spanish moss, lifted its crown above the other trees, and sometimes you'd see a hawk wheeling in the sun. "I bet there're still ivorybills in there," my father would say.

"Really?" I asked.

"Could be. There're places in that swamp nobody's ever been in."

There was just a chance that he was right. Before the extensive logging operations of the late nineteenth century, the floodplains of the great southeastern rivers were prime habitat for this largest and most striking of North American woodpeckers. The ivorybill was uncommon even then, but those who ventured into the deep woods, such men as Audubon and William Bartram, had no trouble distinguishing it from the similar but smaller pileated woodpecker. The plumage of the ivorybill was a glossy blue-black, its prominent beak the color of ivory, and flying from tree to tree it called in what Audubon described as the plaintive tone of a clarinet. By 1941, when I was born, the survival of the species was in doubt. As a child I feared I would never see one, even if I were to spend my life hunting for it, but my father's observation suggested the possibility.

We lived in Darlington, ten miles west of the river. With no one to take me into the swamp I had to settle for the little creek below my house. I never saw even a pileated woodpecker in its woods, but the stream was deep enough for fishing, and it flowed through a cypress bottom. Our side of it was practically my front yard. On summer nights I would sit in the porch swing with my father and ask him what wild animals lived in those woods. He would say, "Ssh. Let's see if we can hear an owl." But after a while he would tell me quietly about fishing in the creek when he was a boy and running barefoot down the same paths I knew to the same swimming holes. And I would ease into sleep upon the murmur of his talking.

Next morning I would go out and sit on the steps in the cool early light and listen to the songs of birds I couldn't name. Though my father was dressed for work when he came out, there was always a chance that he would decide at the last minute that he had time to see if the redbreasts were biting. "You remember what you did with those poles?" he would ask.

"Yessir," and I'd be up and running.

"Better get the hoe too. And see if you can find a can."

There was always the chilly swish of wet broomsedge against my bare legs and sometimes the stinging rake of a briar as we crossed the field toward the creek and went down into that dark cypress bottom. The damp black soil squished between my toes as we dug for bait among the cypress knees. That was almost as much fun as fishing—the suck of the wet clay as you hoed back a clod and spied a thick, blue worm, almost as big around as your little finger, wriggling into the ground.

With three or four nightcrawlers in the can, we came out of the shade upon a wide bend where banked honeysuckle overhung the water and the sun touched the sandy, scalloped bottom. Finding a place to settle, we spent an hour, intent upon our corks as they bobbed against the sweep of the current. At such times I was easily distracted by birds or butterflies or particularly a certain dragonfly that was common in those woods. It was an electric-blue needle of an insect with narrow black wings. Sometimes one would alight on the tip of my pole and I would become so absorbed in the slow pulse of its wings that I would forget my cork. Then my father would say, "Watch your cork, son." The round yellow bobber, jerked almost out of sight in the dark water, jolted me into action, and one nice redbreast with its dark green back and crimson throat was enough to make me want to fish forever. When my father left for work, I stayed behind, watching as he picked his way through the rich black mud of the bottom.

When I was six or seven I began spending weekends in the country with a friend named Freddie McIntosh. Although he and his brothers treated me like a town boy, I loved to go to their house because they lived above a wild stream called Alligator Branch where their father and mine had played together when they were boys. Summer and winter we ranged the woods, fishing and swimming in the shallow, tea-colored creek when the weather was warm and hunting 'coons with a black man named Charlie Ross on cool autumn nights. When the night was unusually cold, down in the forties, say, Charlie built us a fire on a hill above the branch. Then we huddled around the flames as we waited for the dogs to strike. Freddie and his brother knew the voices of their dogs, but only Charlie could name the game they were running.

"Sound like a possum," he would say, or, "Queen got a 'coon."

One night when the dogs barked "treed," Charlie said, "I believe that a cat," and I looked at his dark face in the firelight to see if he was serious.

Freddie and his brother and I were camping on the branch one summer night when suddenly we were startled by the scream of an animal, not far off in the woods. It was utterly wild, a catlike wail of rage and pain. I grabbed Freddie's arm. "What was that?" I asked.

Freddie and his brother laughed. "Sounded kinda like a bobcat," Freddie said, "but it could be a panther."

"Shoot. I bet."

In a slow drawl his brother said, "It could be one. It could come up here from the river. Through Back Swamp."

"There ain't no panthers in the Pee Dee Swamp."

"The heck there ain't," Freddie said. "Son Gandy saw one, one time. Bears too. Cud'n Ben Jolly found bear tracks on the island last winter."

The island was a large tract of land that lay between the river and an oxbow called Lowder's Lake. Ben Jolly and his brothers held deer drives there in the fall, though deer were so scarce in our part of the state that when someone killed a buck people talked about it for days in the barber shops and cafés around the public square. I had heard the talk, but I had never seen a deer. I asked Freddie if there were any on the branch. He said their daddy used to see them when he was a boy. "But they're all in the riverswamp now."

Freddie and his brother called pileated woodpeckers "Indian hens." We saw them often. But even they didn't claim to know anyone who had seen an ivorybill, even in the riverswamp.

"I'd sho like to go in there sometime."

Freddie and his brother laughed. "Shoot, Kilgo, you'd get so lost in there they'd never find you."

"You could take a compass."

"Compass? Compass wouldn't do you no good in the river-swamp. People have to use string."

"String?"

"Yeah. You string it behind you so you can find your way back out. You go in there, you'd see string all over the place."

"Really?"

"Heck yeah. It's deep in there."

When Freddie spent the night with me, I took him down to my creek, but I could never think of anything for us to do. Wherever we went we could hear the sounds of the neighborhood and occasionally through the treetops see the back of a house at the top of the hill. Looking at the creek bottom through his eyes, I noticed stranded Clorox and liquor bottles, the flotsam of high water I'd never paid attention to before.

"Want to go fishing?" I asked one day.

"In that creek?"

"Yeah. It's got fish in it."

"And a lot of other stuff too."

"What?"

"That crap over there. Looks like sewage."

The dead water caught in a bend was coated with scum, and

dirty foam gathered against a log.

"That ain't sewage," I said. "Me and Daddy fish down here. He wouldn't fish down here if it was."

Freddie just laughed.

So instead of fishing we went exploring. I had wandered as far down the creek as the park on the other side of town, but I had never ventured upstream because somewhere beyond the woods was the mill village, and I was afraid of stumbling onto the territory of the rough boys who lived there. But that day Freddie and I not only went upstream, we crossed the creek as well.

A heavily used path led us toward the hill, and sooner than I expected we came to the edge of the woods. There before us was a garbage dump—rusted bed springs and a wet mattress, old radios, cans and a broken doll—the refuse of mean lives, meanly disposed of just out of sight of some back door. Picking our barefooted way around it, we crept up the hill and found ourselves looking into the dirty backyard of a small, unpainted house. Right before us on the ground was something that looked like thrown-out grits, congealed to the form of a pot. We could hear a woman's voice talking to someone inside the house.

"Let's get out of here," I said.

Freddie laughed. "That's where your sewage is coming from."

Soon after that the highway department came and extended the road beside my house into the woods and across the bottom. The loud yellow machines worked all summer long, hammering at the woods and ruining even hills. When they had cleared the roadbed, straight as a yardstick across the bottom, I was startled to see how short the distance was from my yard to the houses on the other side. By the time school started in September, the road spanned the creek. The bridge stood just above the hole where we had fished.

Soon after that my family moved to the other side of town. The creek bottom where I had played and fished receded with the memories of childhood, and I turned to other things. Girls, mostly. Ernest Hemingway has explained the experience as clearly perhaps as anyone. To his friend Bill Smith he wrote, "Guy loves a couple or three streams all his life, loves 'em better than anything in the world—falls in love with a girl and the goddam streams can dry up for all he cares."

If there had been some older man—a ne'er-do-well uncle with a shack on the river or a healthy grandfather who loved to hunt— I might have managed both pursuits. Instead, I was left to the impulses of the crowd I ran with.

During my last two years of college I was preoccupied with a girl who went to school in New Orleans. After graduation I married the girl, moved to New Orleans, and began graduate study in American literature.

For the first time in my life I was too far from Darlington County to go home for a weekend visit. Amid the exotic odors and abrasive accents of that strange city I began to miss the familiar light and weather of the seasons I had known in South Carolina. Some of my professors and most of my fellow graduate students seemed indifferent to country things and contemptuous of the rural South. If the subject of hunting came up, their condescending chuckles reminded me how far I was from home. So it may have been in defense of what I wanted my heritage to mean that I took to the woods again, chasing woodcock in Tangipahoa Parish and warblers in the Bonnet Carré Spillway. The hunting and the bird-watching started at about the same time, but the game didn't matter as long as it led me into the woods.

I was watching birds one day in the woods along a river in Tangipahoa. Though it was only mid-April, the spring was well-advanced, a warm breath from the Gulf bringing swarms of little birds. The treetops, newly leaved, were abuzz with warblers and vireos. By quick, frustrating glimpses I was recognizing for the first time in my life tiny, brightly colored birds that I had known only from the field guide—black-throated blues and black-throated greens, redstarts, and boldly patterned black and yellow hooded warblers. Beneath the canopy I stood, binoculars raised to my eyes, looking straight up, turning in wonder as birds darted about above me.

Suddenly through the general buzz came a call, distant but nasal and emphatic, like a bleat. My heart jumped. I dared not even think *ivorybill!* but its image flashed before me. I *was* next door to Feliciana Parish where Audubon made his painting of the bird. I paused to listen. Merely the possibility, remote as it was, overcame my better judgment. Though I had no clear sense of the direction from which it had come, I struck out toward the deepest part of the woods, and as I walked I found it easy to imagine that the long-haired painter himself was fading into the green recesses up ahead.

I might be walking yet had it not been for the river. In the sunlight on the bank I recovered my equilibrium. I could not have heard an ivorybill, I decided. But I had heard something. Although I was hard at work on my dissertation that spring and had already obtained a position in the English Department at the University of Georgia for the fall, I began to realize that the call that had come to me was my true vocation. Wherever my profession might take me in the years to come, I knew I would follow that elusive woodsman into the riverswamp of my childhood dream, a green place, deep enough for ivorybills, with no far side to come out on.

2
Actual Field Conditions

As creatures of song and flight, birds suggest so powerfully the impulses of the mind and spirit that Adam himself must have made the connection. Even in ancient mythology and fairy tale, according to Marie Louise von Franz, birds stand for "a nearly bodiless entity, an inhabitant of the air, of the wind sphere, which has always been associated with the human psyche." Poets have persisted in the mythological view. Keats' nightingale, Shelley's skylark, Hopkins' kestrel, and Yeats' swans all correspond to something in our nature that refuses to accept mortality and dreams of the freedom of flying. The major weakness in this way of seeing, as any ornithologist will quickly tell you, is its failure to recognize the behavior of birds under actual field conditions.

WHEN I WAS A BOY THERE were men in my hometown who were respected for their knowledge of birds. They were not bird lovers in the usual sense of that term but farmers and foresters who spoke without self-consciousness about such things as declines in the redheaded woodpecker population or the rare occurrence in our area of a painted bunting.

Once, when we were fishing on the creek below our house, my father suddenly gripped me by the shoulder and whispered, "Look!" He put his hand on the back of my head and aimed my gaze toward a ferny spot on the far bank. There, flitting about among the sun-splotched leaves, was a small yellow bird I had never seen before. "That's a prothonotary warbler," he said. The conjunction of that improbable name with the brilliant flame color of its breast seemed marvelous to me.

The first bird I identified on my own was a black and white warbler. I was ten or eleven years old, sitting one morning on a log near the creek, when I spied it in the low canopy overhead. Although I was familiar with the species from an illustration by Louïs Agassiz Fuertes in a set of cards I had ordered from Arm and Hammer Soda, I was not prepared for the precision of zebra striping on a bird so tiny. I ran all the way home, excited by a wild conviction that something had been settled.

What had been settled, I understood much later, was my experience of that particular species. The sight of the bird required a response—I had to do something about it. A camera would have worked—even a gun, I'm afraid, because I wanted to have the bird—but the name alone was enough. Armed only with that, I applied it, ratified the act of seeing, and appropriated the black and white warbler.

Perhaps the obvious way of seizing and holding such moments of delight, especially for one who is able to draw, is by painting the bird. For some reason, that possibility did not occur to me until I was grown. By the time it did, I had devoted several years to avid birding, naming every new species I could find until my fascination with birds was reduced to a mere game of listing, in which the checking off of a species amounts almost to a cancellation of it. As if that weren't bad enough, the game became for me a competition with other such binocular-visioned people.

Then one day on the beach of Sapelo, a barrier island off the coast of Georgia, something happened that changed my way of looking at birds. I was participating in a Christmas bird count with a small group of experienced birders and ornithologists. On Saturday night one of them reported having seen what he thought was a stilt sandpiper on the south end of the beach. Because that species occurs rarely on the South Atlantic coast, most of us needed it for our lists, so early the next morning the whole crowd piled into a couple of vehicles and headed down the strand.

We must have presented quite a spectacle as we climbed from the jeeps—a brigade of birders, wrapped in heavy coats and armed with binoculars, some even with a 'scope and tripod, tramping down an empty winter beach to "get" a sandpiper. According to Roger Tory Peterson's description, the bird is almost indistinguishable at that time of year from dowitchers and lesser yellowlegs. Even the man who had reported seeing it had had trouble confirming identification because it was part of a mixed flock of small shorebirds.

The sun stood before us upon the water, its reflection blazing on the wet sand where the waves reached and retreated, and a cold salt wind was blowing off the ocean. I began to doubt that I would have the patience to sort out a stilt sandpiper from a large flock of sand-colored shorebirds, and I was bothered as well by the legitimacy of my recording it if someone else identified it first.

On the point at the end of the beach hundreds of birds were racing along the edge of the surf; hundreds more lay dozing in the dry sand, their feathers ruffled by the steady wind; and a few big, solitary willets stood here and there like unhappy schoolteachers watching children at recess. I took one look through my binoculars into the glare and realized that I didn't care enough about a stilt sandpiper to bother.

Looking for something to pick up—driftwood, bottle, or shell—I left the crowd and climbed the high dunes. On the other side, between me and the marsh, lay a long, shallow lagoon. It appeared to be connected to the sound at high tide, but now with the ebb it was an isolated pool. A flock of large birds, all of a kind, was wading in it, stretching, preening, and feeding. They were marbled godwits—a species I had seen before—but I grabbed my binoculars anyway and focused on one bird. From that angle the light upon its mottled brown plumage was ideal; I could even detect the flesh-colored base of its recurved bill. Then I lowered the glasses in favor of the whole choreography. There must be fifty of them, I thought, and I marveled at their obedience to the common will that moved them all in one direction, comprehending a dozen little sideshows of casual interaction. I delighted in the repetition of muted color and graceful form, reflected fifty times in blue water.

Suddenly, by a shared impulse the godwits rose crying from the pool and wheeled in an arc above me, their cinnamon wings flashing in the sun. I watched them fly south toward St. Simons, hearing their cries after I could no longer distinguish the flock in the shimmering air.

With the dying away of their cries I sat down on the dune. The other bird-watchers were scattered on the beach below me, still focused on the flock of sandpipers, but I was not ready yet to rejoin them. For I had seen godwits rising in the sun—a glory of godwits crying down upon the marshes—and I felt strangely abandoned. I wanted to grab hold of that moment with both hands, before it faded away with the birds, and keep it; and I wanted to tell my friends on the beach about it so they could see it too. If only I could paint it all, I thought—the strong winter light and the birds' insistent cries. I could at least try, I decided. I would paint it in watercolor, bathed in that light, and those who saw it would feel something of the loneliness I had felt.

Not long after the Christmas count on Sapelo I saw the illustrations by Robert Verity Clem for *The Shorebirds of North America*. They represented exactly the kind of thing I wanted to do. For the next year I studied them as well as the work of Fuertes and George Miksch Sutton, sketched hundreds of birds in the field, and often picked up road-kills to learn anatomy and plumage patterns. It was not mere illustration I sought but a representation of the experience of seeing a particular bird in its habitat, as I had seen the black and white warbler that day on the creek or those godwits rising above me in the sun.

The ornithologist who introduced me to the behavior of birds under actual field conditions was a south Georgia farmer named Calvin Hardy, one of the group on the Christmas count. When I met him on the dock, waiting for the boat to Sapelo, I could see right away that he was different from the rest of us. Big and sturdy, as though cut to a larger pattern than most men, he gave the impression that if something broke he could fix it.

I was not surprised to hear that Calvin was a farmer and a forester. In fact, he reminded me of those men whose interest in birds I had noticed when growing up. Before the weekend was over I learned, partly by talking to him but mostly from a mutual friend, that he was also an airplane pilot and a carpenter of better-than-average skill; that he had published papers on herpetology, mammalogy, and ornithology; that he photographed wildflowers and collected stamps and coins, antique turpentining equipment, and local folklore; and that he lived in an old railroad depot that he had moved two miles from its original site after cutting it in half with a chain saw.

Somehow Calvin and I discovered quickly that each of us had stories the other wanted to hear, so we spent the late night hours of that weekend drinking coffee and talking. By the time we left the island Sunday afternoon, I knew that he, like me, was one of those people who has to do something about birds. Painting, I had just realized, was the thing I would do; Calvin's was science. At that time he was working on the nesting habits of herons and egrets. "Come on down to south Georgia in June," he said, "and we'll go into a rookery."

Most wading birds are colonial nesters. The colony is called a rookery, or by some a heronry. In south Georgia the birds often select lime-sink ponds as nesting sites. As long as a colony site remains undisturbed the birds will return to it year after year until they eventually fill the capacity of the place; an established rookery may contain six different species of wading birds and as many as two thousand nests. Calvin had been going into the rookeries in his part of the state for several years, mainly for the purpose of determining and monitoring fluctuations in the populations of the predominant species—the little blue heron and the cattle egret, the latter an exotic that had made its way across the Atlantic from Africa at the end of the nineteenth century and has since worked its way north to our continent. Though the intruder does not compete for food with native species, Calvin suspected that it was taking over sites formerly held by the little blues.

In May he called to remind me of the invitation. The nesting season would be at its peak in a few weeks, he said; we might find as many as five or six species. I needed no encouragement. The rookery would afford a rare opportunity to photograph and sketch the wading birds in their own bedroom. I could hardly wait.

The morning was already hot when we climbed from the truck and started across a brushy field. Ahead of us stood the woods, quietly shimmering through the heat waves as though nothing remarkable were happening within its shadow. But presently we began to detect a commotion, a murmur of flaps and squawks. As we drew nearer, the trees before us seemed to bloom with white birds. Herons were ascending, reluctantly it appeared, to hover above the canopy, legs a-dangle, and complain at our intrusion. Still nearer, we caught a vague whiff of organic effluvium that grew stronger as we approached the trees.

Beneath the canopy we paused at the edge of what appeared to be not water but a pale green floor; through it rose a thin forest of tupelo gum, red maple, pond cypress, and pine. The flapping activity of the adult birds receded before us to the far reaches of the rookery, and for a moment I could neither see nor hear young birds. After the clamor that had greeted us, the silence seemed unnatural. I thought of alligators, prehistoric submarines cruising noiselessly beneath the green floor, and I felt some reluctance to enter the rookery. Calvin had not mentioned gators to me, but since we were entering their habitat I thought I might ask.

"I wouldn't worry about them," he said. Then he smiled, "But if you do get tangled up with one, remember now that his belly is the soft part."

His smile was no sure sign that he was kidding because he smiled most of the time—so I checked a bit furtively to see that my Randall skinning knife was still securely fastened on my hip. Then I followed him in.

A thick mat of vegetation, streaked and splashed with chalky excrement, lay upon the surface of the pond. Beneath this, the water was a warm chowder. Ten yards out we were waist-deep in it, pushing the surface before us like a buckling rug and releasing smells that engulfed us as we moved.

Calvin was already busy recording data with a pad and a mechanical counter as he moved confidently through the trees. I was dropping behind, still a little conscious of my legs but mainly marveling at the nests—frail platforms, four or five to a tree sometimes, lying in the forks of branches six to eight feet above the water. Looking up from underneath I could see the sky through them, and many of them held clutches of three eggs. By climbing onto the roots of a tree and holding on to the trunk I was able to look into several nests. The eggs were of the palest blue-green, as large as golf balls and oval in form. What astonished me most was the capacity of such slight nests to support their weight.

Many of the nests contained newly hatched chicks, nestled in damp clumps (sometimes around an addled egg), and looking back at me with yellow reptilian eyes. From the number of fledglings standing about on the edges of nests and neighboring branches, I figured that these birds, in their ravenous determination to receive food before their siblings, quickly developed the strong legs that enabled them to climb out of their flimsy quarters. Once out, however, they remained in the immediate vicinity, jostling each other in clumsy sidestep as they awaited the return of their parents with food. Most of the birds we saw were in this stage of development, ineffectual sentinels protesting our presence by gaping and squawking and, in their excitement, sometimes regurgitating or defecating as we passed by or paused to take pictures of them.

Most birds in the fledgling stage are ungainly—hence the tale of the ugly duckling—but few species present a greater contrast between the immature stages and the adult than wading birds. Crowned with ludicrous patches of hairy down, these tailless white creatures seemed badly put together—too much neck, too much leg, and none of it under control. They looked to be in constant danger of toppling from the branches, and occasionally a chick would lose its balance. We saw one hanging upside down, wings fallen open so that the light shone through the membranes, and clutching its perch with the toes of one desperate foot.

I wondered how long the bird could last in that position and how long a gator would take to find it once it had let go. Calvin said he doubted that alligator predation was a significant factor in the mortality of immature birds, though he was sure that the reptiles took an occasional victim as they scavenged the rookery. Just then he pointed out a young bird crawling from the thick gravy at the base of a tree and clambering laboriously up its trunk, using beak, claws, and even wings like some prehistoric creature moving from the amphibian stage through the reptilian to the avian in one heroic action. But I was not moved to admiration. In its mindless determination to survive, the creature seemed hideous to me—but I was hot and filthy, and I had already seen too many birds, too many eggs.

On our way out of the rookery Calvin spied a pair of anhinga chicks perched in their nest about ten feet up and had me stand on his shoulders to photograph them. Their buff down looked as thick as the nap on a baby harp seal, and I had to restrain an impulse to stroke them. After snapping several pictures I lowered the camera to Calvin and embraced the tree to shinny down the trunk. As I glanced over my shoulder at the green surface beneath me, I felt suddenly that I was suspended above the primal generative slime itself, composite of earth, air, fire, and water, secreted from the earth by what Annie Dillard has called "the pressure of fecundity." I clung to the tree, appalled by the terrific energy that digested sticks, eggs, leaves, excrement, even baby birds, and bubbled up a scum of duckweed, releasing in the process a blast of heat and odor. God knows, I thought, what it might produce if it had the time.

"You need some help?" Calvin asked. The question restored my equilibrium. This was after all only a rookery. So I climbed down and followed in his wake toward dry land. As we approached the edge, adult herons and egrets with a clapping and beating of wings began to reclaim the area we had deserted, young birds commenced to clamor again for food, and the rookery resumed its normal business. Give them a wooded lime-sink pond, I thought, and they would do the rest—these ethereal white creatures—by dropping sticks and laying eggs and regurgitating a mash of protein and defecating thousands of times a day. And the result? New egrets, hundreds of them, emerging from the rank miasma to glide like angels upon fields of summer hay or to float upon their individual images in quiet ponds.

Near the edge of the rookery a white egret rose up from a low nest ahead of us and flapped off through the trees. Calvin sensed it was something different, but he resisted a conclusion. In the nest we found a wet, new chick and two eggs, one cracking even as we looked into it. "Snowy egret," he guessed, but the scientist in him required confirmation so we hid and waited for the parent to return.

The most elegant of American wading birds, the snowy is a predominantly coastal species, and we were over a hundred miles inland. Calvin suspected that this might be a nesting record for the interior of the state—he had never found snowies in a rookery before. I shared a little of his excitement, but my thoughts were of a different nature. As wading birds go, the stumpy little cattle egrets we had been observing occupy the lower end of the aesthetic yardstick. Somehow, it seemed to me, that fact had something to do with the evidence we had just seen of the birds' appetite for breeding. I had no trouble envisioning a field of cattle egrets shamelessly engaged in the business of reproduction, but the image of snowy egrets copulating had never before occurred to me.

When the adult returned to the nest we spotted instantly the bright yellow toes on black feet that confirmed Calvin's impression. Grasping a thin branch, the egret seemed to reverse the direction of its wing beats in a frantic effort to balance itself. I couldn't tell which parent this was, but the bird's white flurry in that shadowed place startled me into a vision of a gorgeous male, nuptial plumes aquiver as he climbed the back of a crouching female and held her neck in his beak.

I didn't give much thought to painting that night. As we sat in front of his house, watching purple martins in the heavy twilight, Calvin interpreted the statistics we had gathered, and his eyes sparkled as he recalled various details of our trip. But my skull was filled with a green stew that sloshed when I lay down to sleep, and my imagination struggled with wet wings to climb out of it. If I was praying to the same God who charged egrets with the procreative urge, I didn't see how I could expect much of an audience.

The next morning Calvin took me up in his Taylorcraft, a flying machine of uncertain vintage that reminded me more of a kite than an airplane. He thought he had discovered the general location of a new rookery in the next county and wanted to see if he could verify it from the air. About ten miles west of town, at fifteen hundred feet, he pointed out a cool green spot on the ground that looked exactly like a mint, dropped down onto the patchwork of fields and woods. "Recognize that?" he asked. White specks, brilliant particles against the dark ground, were converging upon the spot and radiating from it in slow, deliberate flight. I felt as though I were looking down through clear water at something going on in another world. The effects of the day before were already beginning to diminish; nothing about the mint-green spot prompted memory of the rookery's reek and clamor. I began to understand the lofty point of view. It was easy up here to ignore rookeries, even to deny the fall of baby birds, and I saw that there might be some chance for the imagination in the clean, cold, blue air.

Then came the hawks. They appeared at first as a dark shape out in front of us. We didn't recognize it immediately, the thing not in flight but falling, and hurtling not away but toward us. Then, for a single instant, we saw clearly *two* birds in clasped union; for that frozen moment they seemed suspended in the force of their own energy. Almost into the prop, they split apart, one blown past the windshield, the other peeling away below. If I had been standing up, my knees would have buckled.

"What was that?" I shouted above the engine.

"Red-tails, weren't they?"

"I mean, what were they doing?"

"What did it look like?"

"You mean they really do it in the air like that?"

"What do you think?" he asked.

But I couldn't answer. I was so exhilarated by that incredible intersection, thinking was out of the question.

On the ground again, I remembered Walt Whitman's poem about the free fall of copulating eagles: "A swirling mass tight grappling,/In tumbling turning clustering loops, straight downward falling." A single, graphic image of what he calls their dalliance, it risks no statement of meaning, evidently because Whitman thought the image was message enough. I agree with his judgment, but I had made closer contact with the birds I saw. Their attractive force clapped me to them. And though the roar of the plane had interrupted their long tumble and blasted them apart, I continue to fall with them, convinced that the whole green earth below was one damned rookery, its power as strong as gravity.

3
A Taste for Game

SOME PEOPLE ARE SURPRISED that Henry David Thoreau in *Walden* advises parents to allow their sons to hunt, but he believed that hunting and fishing were the best ways to introduce a boy to the woods. My father would have said he didn't need a Yankee transcendentalist to tell him that a boy ought to know what it feels like to knock down a bobwhite quail on a covey rise. His own father had seen to that, and when I was old enough he began to teach me.

That tradition in our family became tangible in a twenty-gauge L. C. Smith. The gun had belonged to my grandfather and bore his initials on a brass stockplate. I suspect that my grandfather planned to put the gun in my hands himself at the appropriate time, for I inherited his name as well, but he didn't live long enough to do that. So the gun stood for years in a closet in my parents' room—mine by authority of the stockplate, but forbidden. On special occasions I was allowed to pick it up, only to discover that the gun was too heavy for me to lift and too long to bring to my shoulder. "You've still got some growing to do," my father would say, as he returned it to its corner.

By the time I was twelve, however, I was familiar with every detail of the gun—the fine grain of its walnut stock and forearm, the smooth resistance of its triggers, the writing on its barrels. I had taken it down and reassembled it a hundred times, delighting in the mirror sheen of its bores, the tight snap of its action, the precision of its balance, and I was ready to use it.

After the necessary apprenticeship in firearm safety, my father took me hunting. The dogs were borrowed and the land belonged to an old woman who lived in the country, but as far as I was concerned we were lords of a vast estate. I wasn't even bothered by the light drizzle that day or the failure of the dogs to find many birds. I was carrying my own shotgun.

As evening was closing in, we came out of a field of dead corn and saw the dogs locked on point at the edge of the woods. The bitch Fran had nailed them—you could tell by the way her head was jerked to the left as though the smell of quail had snagged her in mid-stride—and Fritz was backing her, with a serious look on his face as though he expected us to believe that he smelled them too. "They're right in front of Fran," my father said. "Just move on up." I took a tentative step. We had flushed two coveys that afternoon and I was prepared to flinch. "And remember this time to shoot at one bird. You can't kill the whole covey." I noticed the bloody tip of Fran's rigid tail, and took another step, and the covey erupted at my feet. I recovered from the fluttering roar of the rise in time to be confused by the wild scattering of birds, but then I saw one bird clearly. The gun fired, there was a puff of feathers, and feathers drifted down in the heavy air.

My father was pumping my hand as Fritz came up with the bird. It was a rooster, its white throat glowing in the dusk. Now that the shooting was over I didn't know how to act, so I took the warm bird from the dog's mouth without looking at it closely and stuffed it in my pocket. Suddenly my father put his arm around my shoulder and told me that I had made a good shot and that I should be proud of my first bobwhite quail. So I grinned and retrieved the bird from my pocket, and we admired it for a minute in the lingering light. As we turned to leave, I spied the spent shell waxy red in the beaten grass and picked it up and held it to my nose.

To be fair to Thoreau, I have to add that while he approved of hunting and fishing for boys, he assumed that morally sensitive people would outgrow those activities as they developed a responsible attitude toward nature. He himself was a case in point. Having hunted as a boy, he began to "distinguish his proper objects as poet and naturalist"; any man who has in him "the seeds of a better life," he believed, will follow the same course and finally leave his gun and fish-pole behind.

Although I had no idea of becoming either a poet or a naturalist, I gradually stopped hunting after we moved to Georgia. As a graduate student in Louisiana I had hunted quail, ducks, and woodcock—with enthusiasm if not with much frequency—and I had looked forward to continuing that activity in the country around Athens. But good hunting is hard to come by in a new place. Even harder to find is the right person with whom to hunt. After several disappointing experiences I gave up the effort. A year came at last when I didn't go hunting at all. I was about thirty then, settled into a quiet subdivision and teaching Sunday school. The L. C. Smith was retired to a gun rack on the wall, a decorative relic of a family tradition that I didn't see much way of sustaining, and my family and I were living more or less contentedly on butterball turkeys and corn-fed Kansas beef.

In the spring of 1972 I joined a university class in ornithology for a field trip to Sapelo Island. On the way down I noticed with distaste a tall, skinny young man in the back of the van. He was at the center of an admiring group who seemed to be impressed because he was drinking beer in defiance of a prohibition against alcohol on a university vehicle, and they laughed at everything he said. I had trouble understanding what he was doing in such a class. Most of the students were wildlife biology majors for whom ornithology was a required course, but I could see nothing in their hero to indicate an affinity for anything natural.

With his undercut chin and prominent Adam's apple, his wavy dark hair and the black caterpillar of a mustache on his lip, he reminded me of the bass singer in a gospel quartet. He had that feigned apologetic look that you see in the eyes of people who are used to being in trouble, and he was telling his jokes and stories in a soft falsetto drawl. His long body was folded into a jackknife on the crowded back seat, and the only young woman in the class was snuggled in tight beside him. Now and then he would interrupt one of his own stories to whisper in her ear. She would giggle or slap him lightly on the arm, and all of his buddies would roar. I resented her attraction to him. She appeared to be an intelligent person, whereas he in his maroon double-knit trousers was the original of every drummer who ever hit the main drag of a south Georgia town.

But it's a long way from Athens to Sapelo. I was sitting two rows forward of the back-seat commotion. In self-defense I began talking to the student next to me. Eventually the conversation turned to hunting; soon I was interrupted by a tap on the shoulder. The long-legged fellow had overheard us: "You like to hunt, p'fesser?"

For some reason I said yes.

"What? Ducks? You need to come with me sometimes. I can take you to a place where them summer ducks and mallets fall out of the sky by the hunerds."

—*Mallets?*

"Farm down in Greene County where I been trapping beaver. If you want to go, we'll go."

I was finding it hard to believe that this clown was a hunter and a trapper. I had always been suspicious of casual invitations and the extravagant claims that usually accompany them. Besides that I had never liked to hunt with strangers. Then he twisted his amazing body into an imitation of a duck coming in, extended his neck, set his wings, and quacked. Exactly like a "mallet." When I stopped laughing, I shook his hand and promised I would take him up on his invitation when the season opened in November. He said, "Good. My name's Wayne Purvis. Have a beer," and produced a tall one from a paper sack beneath his seat.

Purvis picked me up in his long red Pontiac Bonneville at four-thirty on the opening morning of duck season. The first cold front of the fall was right on time, and he was excited. Bad weather up north should have pushed some big ducks down, he said; he couldn't hardly wait. When we reached the farm, he pulled off the highway, stopped before a fastened gate, and turned the headlights off. "Don't like people to see me coming in here. They might get the idea there's a good beaver pond around."

As Purvis struggled with the latch, the wide, dark fields beyond him heaved against the paling sky like the chest of a man sleeping. Upon the low crest stood two dark silos, for some reason a little threatening, and I could smell cattle in the cold night air.

Directly across the river, Purvis had told me, was the place where university biologists had begun the deer restocking program in the Piedmont. By the turn of the century, rural poverty and the heavy planting of cotton had reduced the population to a riverswamp remnant and brought about the extirpation of beavers. Even now, after twenty years of cattle production and pine plantations, the Oconee River still ran muddy from the erosion of red clay. But the deer and beaver were coming back. In fifteen

years, the fifty-eight animals released by the biologists had produced one of the largest herds in the state, and deer hunting had
become the most popular field activity in the Georgia Piedmont.
At the same time the beaver population was increasing at such a
rate through the Oconee River drainage that the animal had become a pest. Purvis had obtained hunting rights on this land, he
told me, in exchange for his trapping beavers for the owner.
Meanwhile, the beavers were creating vital nesting habitat for
wood ducks and roost ponds for wintering flocks of mallards. Until he had some success, Purvis said, we'd have excellent duck
shooting. "And they're tough little sonofabitches to get rid of," he
grinned.

As Purvis nosed his atrocious automobile along a narrow woods
road, a big doe hurtled across the swinging beam of the headlights. "This place is crawling with them," he said. "You want to
kill a deer, this here's the place to do it." But I didn't want to kill
a deer, or any other mammal that walks around the woods with a
heart and liver as big as my own. Taking careful aim from a tree
at such a creature seemed more like sniping than hunting. Besides that, I thought most deer hunters were the kind of people
who shoot road signs and leave their garbage in the woods. I had
even heard about a man from Atlanta who had come into a checking station the year before with some farmer's old goat shot neatly
through the neck and proudly showed off its curl of horn. If most
were not that bad, the national forests were crowded nevertheless
with people who regarded hunting as an excuse to shoot their rifles. Among these were a few each year who managed to mistake
cows and even other people for a white-tail buck. I wanted no part
of it.

When we got out of the car, Purvis led me through the dark

woods to the edge of the water. We climbed into our waders and loaded our guns. The little L. C. Smith was not designed for ducks, but it was the only gun I owned; Purvis was shooting a big autoloader.

"You head straight out yonder in them trees and find you a place to stand. I'm going up the pond a little piece. They ought to be coming any time now."

I looked out upon the water. Though the eastern sky was growing lighter, the pond itself was still and dark. I was cold and could see my breath. I didn't want to enter it. "Where?" I asked.

"Be careful not to step in a beaver run." With that he disappeared. I listened to his quiet sloshing until I couldn't hear it any longer. When all was quiet again, I stepped into the water, disturbing the mist that played on the dark surface. The bottom seemed firm at first, but it became soft as I moved out from the bank. When I was waist-deep, the pressure of the water glued my waders to my legs like cold skin, and I was soon fighting against the suck of the mud. Once, pulling my foot free, I struck my shin against a submerged log and nearly fell. Without a snag to grab I tottered for a long doubtful moment, holding my gun aloft and thrashing the air with my free arm.

Going fast and slow at the same time, as an old Cajun once told a friend of mine, explaining to him how to walk in a marsh, I crossed an expanse of open water. The bleached trunks of dead trees stood in front of me glimmering in the dark. When at last I reached them, I was soaked with sweat inside my insulated one-piece, and my knees were weak from struggling against the water and the sticks and the mud. I found a stout tree and leaned against it and lit a cigarette.

There is no color in a winter beaver pond. In the darkness just before first light the place seems dead. The erratic low hooting of a great horned owl from a distant ridge somehow deepens the quietness. You notice the pale tree trunks nearby and maybe a peeled stick floating on the water. With the first sharp chirp of a winter wren, the background of dead grass begins to emerge, revealing by contrast the dark hovel of a beaver lodge. Behind you a beaver slaps the surface with its tail. The noise sounds like a country ham hitting the water. You wonder what you look like to the beaver, what it thinks you're doing there, an intruder in its habitat. You don't know, either. You look at the sky. The day is breaking not only upon your face but coming through the windows of your eyes, touching interior corners. And with the breaking of that light the wood ducks squeal, at first a wee whistling from far up the river. You tighten your grip on your gun and thumb the safety. The cries grow louder, insistent now, urgent, like the panicked calling of something that's trying to find its way in a fog. You raise your gun to half-port.

I had been duck hunting from time to time through the years, but I had never seen as many wood ducks as I saw that morning. They came in waves, in squadrons of eight and ten, flaring suddenly against the sky, twisting and tumbling through the branches of dead trees, and pitching onto the water all around me. They came so fast, swinging in against a dark background, that I had no chance to shoot. I caught the splash and sudden glide of a drake and raised my gun to shoot as it flushed, but it disappeared against the darkness when it rose.

I had never killed a wood duck drake, and I wanted one badly, wanted to grasp that color and hold its handsome form in my hand. It didn't occur to me to wonder what I might do with it. I just wanted to have it, as I had wanted many times to catch a bird in my binoculars, rush its blurred image into focus and see the color of its eye. But I wanted the wood duck more.

Purvis shot twice and I looked up. He shot again, but no birds came my way. When I had almost concluded that the brief flight was over, a pair came in behind me, swung by and hooked hard into my face. The lead duck was settling on the water when I hit the other. I missed on the second barrel, but one bird was down, heaped feathers on the gray water and much smaller than it had appeared when it flared against the sky. As I waded toward it, the black and white bars on its flank shone in the half-light; I knew it was a drake. It was as dry as paper when I picked it up. For a moment or two I stood there holding it in my hand.

I lifted it up to take advantage of the light. The heavy pride of its crest and the dramatic pattern of its head engaged my eye and hand more insistently than any bird I'd ever seen. I began to understand why I had come hunting. I would paint this bird as soon as I got home—not in propitiation for having shot it but to appropriate in an act of praise the simple fact that such extravagant beauty exists in the wild, wholly independent of us and our needs.

I admired the crested black head with its white warpaint on cheek and throat and the large, round, scarlet eye and began mixing colors in my mind. How would I find those depths of burgundy or make the irridescence of its scapulars and speculum? At the base of the tail on either side there was a spray of color I'd never seen on any palette. I might avoid the problem of color altogether, of course, by painting the ducks in flight, as I had just seen them, flaring in the early light. But that would reduce the bird to a silhouette. I was after color. I turned it over in my hand and caught the small flash of irridescent purple along its crest.

The thick plumage of its belly was soaked, and a crimson stain was spreading slowly among the wet feathers.

Once when I was a child I found a dead woodcock on the sidewalk of our street. I squatted down, fascinated by the subtle browns of its plumage, the variety of umbers and siennas, and delighted by its improbable head with its big black eyes at the top. But when I picked it up, ants swarmed from its feathers all over my hand and I dropped it quickly, disgusted. Now with the dead duck in my hand I thought I could understand why people go to taxidermists. But I couldn't remember seeing a single mounted bird that hadn't looked more sadly dead than the one I was holding. If my hand had not been so cold with blood and pond water, I might have lifted it open and hoped for a miracle.

Instead, I spread one of the wings and held it so that the speculum like a mirror would catch the weak light. For all its boldness of color and pattern, this wood duck was finally a handful of something to eat, a plump breast of dark red meat. I tucked it into my game bag, taking care not to ruffle its plumage, realizing at the same time that in order to eat it I would have to dress it first. How strange the language is. The bird was already dressed, if anything ever was. The right word for preparing it for the pot would have to be *undress*, or *divest*, or *denude*. I would have to tear the feathers away, the lovely vermiculated gold of the flanks. I would have to snatch out the tail, cut off the head and wings and the leathery yellow feet.

Purvis called to me to come there. I found him above the next beaver dam, standing in knee-deep water, bent forward and sniffing the air. As I approached him, I stepped into a stream of foul air that nearly gagged me.

"What in the hell is *that*?"

"My Conibear."

"Your *what*?"

"Beaver trap. That I lost last month. I looked all over this pond for that damn thing."

He began smelling his way down the nauseating trail until he came to its source. At the same time I backed away to shouting distance, gasping for clean air. When I was able to breathe again, I saw Purvis kneeling in the shallows, his arms elbow-deep and groping. Then with both hands he lifted the streaming contraption from the water. From where I stood something looked glued to it. I called out, "What are you going to do with that thing?" Either he didn't hear me clearly or was too puzzled by the question to answer. At any rate, he ignored me and commenced scraping at the trap with a stick. The wind shifted and I caught a mouthful of corrupt air and almost vomited. But Purvis, engulfed by a dense cloud of it, continued to work.

"How can you stand that?"

This time he looked up, his expression as bland as the face of a cow. "What? This? Shit, I could eat a Big Mac right now."

In spite of the weather we rode back to town with the windows down. The cold wind blew in my face, but it was not cold enough or strong enough to cleanse my nose and mouth of the corruption I had tasted. When we passed a convenience store, Purvis asked if I wanted to stop and get something to eat, but I declined the offer. I didn't know when I might be hungry again.

Though Thoreau confessed once to ranging the woods like a half-starved hound, famished for any wild meat, he was convinced also, he said, that something about the imagination will not be reconciled to flesh and fat. At that moment I agreed. The duck I

had shot was as dead as that beaver, flesh and fat, and the anticipation of its dark, gamey savor was offensive to my palate.

Then the duck flared before me again, spread and splayed,
sculling the air with its wings, and I remembered what it had felt
like to know in the grip and swing of the gun that I was on him.
And then the widening ripples on the water as the cries of the hen
grew fainter and fainter. Something in that moment—some pred-
atory aliveness, intense and concentrated—seemed worth living
for. But if I were going to do it again I knew I had better learn to
eat duck; though flesh and fat at that moment were not appealing,
more sickening still was the furtive disposal of game in a garbage
can. My imagination would just have to take care of itself.

When I got home, I took the wood duck and cut off its head and
wings and feet, plucked its feathers and cleaned its abdominal
cavity. After dumping its parts into a brown paper sack, I
wrapped the dark red breast in paper. I wrapped it tightly so that
no air could get into it, and then I placed it in the freezer.

4
Red Gods

Here and there you will still find a man with Indian blood in his veins.

Henry David Thoreau, *Journal*

WAYNE PURVIS MOVED TO Alabama soon after I began hunting with him. One morning just before he left, as we were driving down to the farm in Greene County, Purvis said, "They's two things I want to do before I leave." We came over the top of the last hill and saw below us in moonlight the great bend of the Oconee River, cradling the dark fields where we hunted. "One is get you permission to hunt down here. And one is to get you and Billy Claypoole together. I need to get him in down here too. That way y'all can hunt together." So Purvis arranged for this Billy Claypoole to meet us at a roost pond one afternoon that week.

We arrived at the place before he did and pulled onto a logging road. It was too rutted and muddy to drive so we walked it for a mile through the woods, carrying our chestwaders over our shoulders. For a while the woods was a monotonous stand of young planted pines. Then the plantation opened suddenly upon a ruined landscape of stumps and broken trunks and strewn pinetops. The road ended in a logging flat on the far side of the cut-over. Below us lay a cattail marsh. We descended the hill to its edge, climbed into our waders, and sat down on the upturned bottom of an old boat to wait for Billy Claypoole. From where we sat the flat above us was a wide gap in the tree line. I kept looking up, expecting to see a figure coming over the crest, but the gap remained empty. The sun went down behind the hill, leaving a winter-orange afterglow.

*   *   *

I knew that this Claypoole was a graduate student in wildlife biology, but if Purvis had told me anything else about him I must not have been paying attention. The likelihood of my hunting with him more than a time or two after this seemed small, for I had met few men through the years whose attitudes were compatible enough with my own for us to enjoy each other's company in the field. Against all probability, Purvis and I liked each other, but I wasn't optimistic about getting along with one of his random friends.

"Do you think he's coming?" I asked.

"He'll be here."

"What time did you tell him?" Since federal regulations prohibit the shooting of ducks after official sunset, I was anxious to get into the water. Most days wood ducks wait until twilight to come into roost; if we were going to get any shooting at all we needed to be in position to take advantage of the few early arrivals.

"We don't have long," I added. "Unless y'all want to shoot after quitting time."

Purvis grinned. "I've killed a world of ducks in my life and I ain't found one yet that was wearing a wristwatch. He'll be here in time to get his limit."

Purvis was less concerned about shooting hours than I was. I assumed he meant that the clock didn't matter to Claypoole either, but I didn't want to ask.

I walked down to the edge of the water. Beyond the field of cattails lay a smoky haze of alder. That was where the woodies would be bedding down. To be in a position to shoot we would have to cross the pond. A light wind stirred the cattails, causing them to rustle, and blackbirds came funnelling out of the empty sky to roost among the stalks. There was a sudden rush of wings, ripping the air above our heads, but the ducks came in so fast we didn't see them.

"I'm going on, Wayne."

"Here he comes now," Purvis said.

I looked around in time to see him at the top of the hill. For the space of two steps he was silhouetted against the bleak orange glow. Then he was down the slope and coming toward us. He was already wearing his waders, and his shotgun hung from a sling over his shoulder, but he walked with an easy grace. I could tell by the dead-leaf tones of his camouflage clothes that he had spent much time in the woods. He was wearing a shapeless felt hat of no particular color. When he took it off, a heavy lock of black hair fell across his forehead. His eyes were black too, smiling straight into my own, and the grip of his big hand was strong. "I'm Billy Claypoole," he said. Then he laughed. "Y'all want to go hunting or sit here talking all night?"

Purvis moved to Alabama a few days after that, leaving to Billy and me his hunting rights on the farm in Greene County and each of us to the other. The hunting didn't come to much. Cold weather had pushed the wood ducks south, and mallards are never reliable on Piedmont beaver ponds. But we went anyway. Billy lived halfway between my house and the farm, so I would stop at his place and transfer my gear to his pickup. By daylight we would be in the water, breaking ice with our knees as we waded out, opening holes big enough for six or eight decoys, and watching the empty, gray sky until eight o'clock or so. Occasionally, one of us killed a duck—usually Billy. Afterwards we would collapse on the bank, exhausted and often wet, and thaw out with a thermos of coffee.

One cold morning Billy came out of the pond with ripped waders, one foot close to frostbite. As we sat massaging life back into his toes, he spoke with envious appreciation of the complex heating-cooling system in polar bears that enables them to swim for hours in arctic seas. His explanation was so specific that I figured he must have recently taken a test on the subject, but several days later he explained in just as much detail the function of fire in the life of the longleaf pine, and on another occasion he told me about studies that had been done on the failure of feral dogs to rear young in the wild. I began to believe that he knew more about natural history than anyone I had ever met. It was a special kind of knowledge—not mere scholarly expertise in a particular discipline but the deep understanding of one who loves, and he wanted me to share his sense of wonder. Describing his work with sea turtles on the Georgia coast, he said that loggerheads heave themselves onto dark beaches not just from the Atlantic surf but out of the depths of evolution itself. "You ought to look one in the eye sometime."

I said I'd love to.

"We'll go down to Cumberland this summer," he promised.

One morning as we were coming out of the pond, we spotted a flock of mallards, a small group flying high, but Billy was able to turn them with a call. A solitary duck was following the flock, wheeling as the others wheeled but not a part of the formation. Its wings flashed silver in the sun. It was a black duck. After they were gone and we had climbed onto the bank, Billy asked me if I had noticed the black.

"It took me a minute to realize what it was," I said. "I wasn't expecting to see one around here."

"You don't see many," Billy said. "They've got too much class to be common. They don't even like to mingle with mallards. Did you see how that one was keeping to himself? He knows he's the ultimate duck. I love them."

On our way back to the truck that day we came upon a place where a deer had bedded down—a rounded spot of matted vegetation that somehow, even among the brambles and broomsedge, looked cozy. Billy knelt and placed his palm on the bent grass. Then he leaned forward and sniffed.

"When a rabbit makes a form like that," I said, "people used to call it a meaze. I don't know whether they had a name for a deer bed or not."

"Have you ever lain down in one, Jim?" Billy asked.

"Oh sure," I said. "I used to do it all the time."

He didn't laugh. "Try it."

It felt strange, but I got down on my hands and knees.

"Now you can see what a buck sees when he's bedded down," Billy said.

I looked all around.

"Except for one thing," he continued. "You aren't in a resting position. Make yourself comfortable."

So I lay down on my back and saw the sky. Then I turned and lay on my side and saw stems of grass. Finally, I flopped over on my stomach.

"See," Billy said. "You can't rest and be alert at the same time. But a deer can. It's worth knowing."

Wayne Purvis had once accounted for Billy's exceptional skill as a hunter by a reference to Indian blood. I had assumed that he was using that as a metaphor, but the more I hunted with Billy the more I wondered if he might really be half Creek or Cherokee. By the end of duck season I felt that I knew him well enough to ask how a person of his southern Scotch-Irish lineage had acquired such dark eyes and straight black hair. With just a hint of a smile he claimed a measure of Choctaw blood. I thought a little black duck might be mixed in too, but I decided not to mention it.

We went to the pond on the last day of the season. Mild weather had thawed the ice, but the thermometer was dropping again. The light came slow and thin, just the way you want it, but we saw no ducks. After an hour it began to rain. That was all I needed to call it quits. I wanted to get warm and dry as soon as possible, but as we came splashing out of the shallows Billy said, "Now. Let's go hunting." To my puzzled expression he explained that the ducks must still be on the river; we had a canoe and the rest of the day to find them—what more could we want?

The Appalachee is a tributary of the Oconee. Two hours later we were on it, drifting in a cold drizzle. Billy insisted that I sit in the bow until I killed a duck, but in three miles we saw no more than we had at the pond. I looked back to complain about the misery of our situation. Billy's green Stetson was soaked dark and rain was dripping from the brim, but his expression was serene and confident so I changed my mind and went back to watching the river.

From the place where we put in, the river had run deep and wide between steep hills, but now the hills gave way to a broad floodplain, and the channel began to unravel into a confusion of shallow streams. Sometimes at a fork we made the wrong decision and eventually scraped sandy bottom. Then we would get out and drag the canoe until we found water deep enough to float us. Often our way was blocked by brush piles and fallen trees; several times we had to portage. Amid those obstacles I lost interest in hunting and concerned myself with the problems of finding our way, but Billy saw that we were in a likely place for ducks. When we were afloat again he insisted that I use his Browning. If we got any shots, he said, I'd probably need the full choke. So we exchanged guns. Without blueing or varnish, his was worn by long use to its essential function. It felt awkward in my hands after the delicate little Smith, heavy and ungainly, and I wondered whether I could manage it comfortably enough to hit a duck.

Billy spied them first. We were swinging into a bend. He whispered, "Ducks, Jim!" and I saw them, three mallard drakes dozing on a spit of sand beneath the overhanging roots of a sycamore. "*Shoot*," he begged, and the ducks jumped into flight. Before I could take account of what was happening, the Browning fired, a duck was rolling in the current, and I was pulling on another. It was already far downstream, but I could see the metallic green of its head shining clearly in the rain-light, and again the Browning seemed to act of its own accord.

We overtook the fallen ducks, and I lifted them from the water as we drifted by. Billy said, "Let's have some coffee," and ruddered the canoe alongside the bank. When we climbed out, he clapped me on the shoulder and shook my hand. "Well done, partner." Opening his thermos, he splashed a swallow on the wet sand. "For the red gods," he smiled. He filled the cup and handed it to me. We sat on a log and talked about the flush. I offered my impressions and he countered with his until we had it right. Then we sat quietly, passing the cup between us and watching the clay-colored river slide by. Not having heard of red gods, I assumed that Billy had made up the term himself, but he said no; he'd found it in a poem by Rudyard Kipling. He couldn't remember the title, but there was something in it about going by canoe to a place of spruce and starlight and finding a smoky Indian standing by a fire.

"I recognize the dream," I said. "It's a longing some people have for a place that's clean and cold and wild. Kind of hard to go looking for it though, if you have to worry about getting home in time for supper."

"Suppertime didn't bother Ben Lilly."

"Who's Ben Lilly?"

"He was an old bear hunter from Louisiana. He was lying around the house one day and his wife told him, since he loved to hunt so much why didn't he go shoot the hen hawk that was getting her chickens. So he picked up his gun and walked out and didn't come back for two years."

Billy and I both laughed.

"She asked him where he'd been, he said that hawk just kept on flying."

"You reckon he found the Indian?"

"He found him."

I stood up. "I wonder if he's still out there? The Indian, I mean."

"I think what you have to do now is let him find you."

Billy refused to sit in the front of the canoe, said he enjoyed watching me shoot more than killing ducks himself. Somehow I knew he meant it, so without protesting strongly I resumed the forward position. We soon came upon another flock of mallards.

It was a large group and they flushed well before we floated into gun range, but one straggler remained, a drake, skulking close against the bank. It jumped as we were upon it, ascending straight up and seeming to hover for a moment in the space between the arching branches overhead. I thought it was too high but shot anyway, nearly toppling over backwards in the canoe. The duck planed away beyond the trees, unscathed as far as I could tell. But Billy said, "Good shot," and sculled the canoe against the bank.

"What are you doing? I didn't hit that duck."

"The hell you didn't. That duck is down." He was already stepping from the canoe into the waist-deep water. "Tie up and come on. We can find that duck."

I had known Billy to spend as much as two hours looking for a crippled bird, but I was sure I had missed this one and saw no reason to waste time in a futile search. I had no idea what time it was nor how far we had to go before we reached the bridge where I had left my car. I didn't think Billy did either. But he had already disappeared into the gray woods. I climbed reluctantly from the canoe and tied it up to a root, clambered onto the bank and entered the woods.

Not knowing which way Billy had gone, I made a wide, perfunctory circle. Even if the duck was down, we had so slight a chance of finding it I hardly bothered to look. As I turned back toward the river, Billy whistled. He was somewhere off to my right, probably within the circle I had made. I found him standing on a bar of sand among sycamores and river birches. His face in that light was as brown as a dead leaf and just as noncommittal.

"What?" I asked.

"You didn't find it?"

"How could I find it when I didn't hit it?"

"Did you come by this way?"

"No. I swung way around yonder."

"Wonder who made those tracks?" he asked, pointing to his left.

The impressions were deep and clean in the wet sand. I didn't have to step into them to know that my boots would fit. "I guess I must have."

"Wonder how you missed this duck then?"

My eyes followed his. Between his feet lay the mallard, its neck and wings extended as though it had expired upon crash-landing. "I'll be damned."

"Seems freshly killed, too," he said.

"I'll be damned if I know how I hit that thing. What made you so sure?"

"He dropped his landing gear. I knew he was hit."

The mallard was mature and deeply colored, and its feathers were unruffled. Thinking that I might have it mounted, I removed my insulated underjacket and wrapped it carefully, cradling it like a baby as we returned to the canoe.

In the time it had taken us to find the duck, the afternoon seemed to have changed to early evening. The weak light of the rainy day was gathered upon the face of the river, draining the woods, so that we floated through a wet, deepening twilight.

"How far do you think it is to the bridge?" I asked.

"Probably not too far now. Jim, see where that channel comes in on the right up there? Might be ducks behind that bank, so be ready."

"You don't have a watch do you?"

"Ssh. Be quiet now," he whispered.

There were no ducks behind the bank, but the volume of the tributary stream made a difference in our speed, I thought, lifting us more quickly toward the bridge.

The iron structure rose in my mind, as skeletal as the Erector-Set bridges I had built as a child. Back in the twenties, when the bridge was new, it must have looked brightly optimistic to the farmers who crossed it on their way to the cotton gin. But it was rusted now and disappointed, and the red clay road was badly rutted and washed. I had been a little concerned all afternoon about leaving my car in such a remote place; now I was more anxious than ever to reach the bridge. If we had to portage around many more fallen logs, we would not get there before dark; if the main channel decided to divide itself again into rivulets too shallow to float us, we would be even later.

A flight of ducks came whistling up the river, too high to shoot.

"You know what we ought to do, Jim? We ought to camp. Right here. This place is going to be alive with ducks in the morning."

I didn't think he was serious. "Yeah," I said, "if we had a tent and sleeping bags."

"We don't need a tent. It's stopped raining. We can eat one of the ducks."

"It's going to get cold tonight, Billy. It's already cold."

"Don't you have matches?"

Maybe he *was* serious. Suddenly I was annoyed by his indifference to our situation. Jane was taking it for granted that I would be home before bedtime, and I was responding to that expectation by concentrating on the bridge. To me it was an exit ramp from the river, a last chance to get off and go home before drifting into a darkening maze of uncharted streams. But Billy didn't care whether we got to the bridge before dark or not. He didn't even care if there was a bridge. Because there was something wild in him, I realized—some part of him not yet domesticated, maverick and free. I thought of his wife Martha. She was a quiet, sweet-natured woman. In the short time I had known them I had been surprised that she would so easily allow him freedom to range the woods and riverbottoms and the lonely county roads. Married men were not supposed to have such freedom. I didn't. I wondered what my wife would say if we spent the night in the woods. Suddenly I liked the idea of a campfire beside the dark river, of dark meat feeding the fire with fat. It wasn't Billy I was annoyed with, it was Jane, expecting me home before bedtime.

"How were you planning to let Martha know?" I asked.

"You see a phone booth anywhere?" Then he laughed. "We'll do it another time."

There was an island up ahead, a dark looming that parted the river like the prow of a ship. The left channel was narrow, but it seemed deeper and swifter than the other so we guided the canoe in that direction. But the island was not an island, and the current became sluggish and slowed; presently it ceased moving altogether and we found ourselves sitting on a little pond listening to the chirps of birds going to bed and the steady rush of a small waterfall that we knew was a beaver dam.

"Now what?" I asked, as though the Appalachee River was Billy's fault.

He chuckled. "Appalachee can be a bitch, can't she?"

I was too tired to respond.

We paddled over to the bank and climbed out and went among the ghostly sycamores in search of the lost channel. Sooner than I expected we came upon a strong current that shimmered in the gathering dark. Hating the thought of picking up the canoe again, even for so short a distance, I said, "Wait a minute. Let me smoke a cigarette first."

So we were standing by the river, and the last of the light was going fast, and something came flying upstream. It was flying heavily at treetop level on strong wings, and it was big and dark. Turning as it passed overhead, Billy lifted the brim of his dark green Stetson, but I couldn't tell whether he was saluting the bird or merely trying to get a better look. When it was gone, he removed his hat, and, combing back his heavy black hair with wet fingers, he looked at me and smiled. It was a smile of exaltation, so blessed that I couldn't speak. I thought *eagle*, but I was afraid that if I named it, and it was one, the suction of its wake would reverse the flow of the river and draw us after it. I said, "What was that, Billy?"

"It was beautiful, wasn't it?" he said.

Afloat on the current again, I sat, blank and listless, allowing Billy to do the work. He didn't have much to do, as it turned out. A couple of bends and there was the bridge, its dark girders arching above us like a black skeleton in the dark.

5
Worthy Blood

SOMETIME DURING THE FIRST nine months or so that I knew Billy Claypoole I must have expressed to him my dismay at the growing numbers of ill-mannered hunters who were crowding into the woods to kill deer. The situation had become so bad in northeast Georgia that on opening day of the season the predawn highways would be lined bumper-to-bumper for miles with four-wheel drives and jacked-up mudhogs. I probably even said I wouldn't be caught dead in that traffic myself. Or something like that. If I had, Billy must not have been paying attention because he said one day in October that the time had come to scout the farm in Greene County.

"I don't even own a rifle," I protested.

"I got one you can use."

"I wouldn't know where to start."

"That's why we're going to Greene County."

So I had to confess that I wasn't sure I really wanted to kill a deer. Yet there had been a time when I could have dreamed of no better thing. As a child in Darlington, I was aware from an early age that people were hunting deer in the Pee Dee River Swamp. If I felt no envious longing to do that myself, it was not because the activity was unavailable to my father and me, but simply because I assumed that hunting deer, like shaving and drinking whiskey, was something that only grown men did. In the barbershop one day I heard different.

Having recently graduated from the booster seat that the barber placed across the arms of the chair for small boys, I was old enough to go into the shop alone. But I was still having my hair cut by Watt Brown, the gentle old black man who owned the barbershop and cut the hair of all the little boys. It would be another two or three years yet before I would be bold enough to choose the younger barber who was preferred by teenagers. So I was sunk deep in the upholstery of Watt Brown's chair when I heard a man in the chair next to me talking about a deer drive. I couldn't tell whether or not he was someone I knew because his face was swathed in steaming towels. But I paid attention because he was speaking of deer and of a boy about my age. The boy's name was Pete Brockington. Though his family owned a large tract of riverbottom land, that didn't make it easier for me to accept what I was hearing because Pete was a year behind me in school.

"Yep," the voice was saying, "his first buck. Nice one, too. Seven points. And I mean that was one more happy young man, hear? When Gus and Harry and them put blood on his face, ol' Pete just grinned his way through it. Wouldn't wash his face for the rest of the day."

A man perched high on the shoeshine stand said, "I'd love to have seen his mama when they took him home."

"Mildred's been through it before," the voice said. "Pete's the baby, you know."

That was not the first time I'd heard of the practice of initiating a hunter by bathing his face in the blood of his first buck. There were not many swamp hunters in Darlington, but those who were observed the ritual. That too was something I had grown up knowing. What I had not known was that it could happen to a boy. A little boy.

Watt Brown had a ritual of his own. At the end of each haircut, after a generous application of hair tonic, Watt would cup his sweet-smelling hand over the boy's nose and hold it there until the child was almost reeling from the alcoholic fumes. I had outgrown that along with the booster seat, but that was a trivial rite of passage compared to killing a deer. Grown men were talking about Pete Brockington in the same tone they used to speak of some particular high school football hero whose play had won the game the night before.

As Watt rubbed the tonic into my hair, I was hoping mightily that he would remember that I had outgrown the hand. The voice in the chair next to me said, "That was the only buck we got, too."

"Be at my house around three," Billy said. "Purvis had a couple of tree stands down there. We'll see if we can find them."

It was a blue October afternoon, the kind sports announcers call a perfect day for football, warm enough for droning bees and spiders and clusters of sulphur butterflies. As we approached the woods, the foliage seemed as green as summer, but among the trees the leaves were gold against the sun and filtered a golden light. Billy talked about deer. "The bucks are just now starting to rut," he said, "but we need some cold weather." Before long he stopped and pointed out a spot on the ground, about the size of a large plate, where the leaves had been raked back to expose bare dirt. "See, that's a scrape."

I didn't know what a scrape was.

"That's the rutting sign of a buck. He usually makes them under a leafy branch like this." The branch was chest-high; Billy caught it in his hand. "See how he's broken these twigs off? He marks the leaves with scent from a gland on his forehead. Then he rubs his tarsal glands together and urinates over them to make the scrape. Telling the ladies there's a man in the neighborhood. We'll probably find some more on down the ridge."

"How many does he make?" I asked.

"He'll have a line of them through his territory."

"Why don't people just put their stands up over the scrapes then?"

"A lot of people do."

"It must not be that easy. I know a man who has been hunting deer for five years—I mean hard—and he hasn't killed one yet."

"You know why that is, Jim? It's because most people don't realize that a deer is an individual creature. They expect all deer to behave the same way all the time. Individual animals are not like that, any more than we are. A buck bedded down in a thicket is constantly processing a world of information that we aren't even aware of, but he still can't decide whether he wants to eat acorns or look for a doe or stay put for a while longer."

"There must be probabilities though," I said.

"There are. But only one thing you can count on. You can be sure that a buck is always going to act like a buck, which means that he doesn't even know himself what he's going to do until he does it. Most of the time though, it's going to be in favor of survival."

"How do you hunt them, then?" I asked.

"It's sort of like a dance. Only you let the buck do the leading."

That afternoon was much more than a seminar in reading deer sign; through Billy's eyes I saw that a deer inhabits a different world from the one measured by our dull perceptions. It may coincide with what we see—hill, sky, and water—and suffer the same weather, but it disposes those elements in an order that most people never glimpse. Because Billy was attuned to that world, he moved differently in the woods from the way he did at other times; he moved with a stillness not only of physical gesture but of attitude as well. Walking behind him, I tried to imitate it, measuring my steps by his, but I missed the attitude. At one point he stopped, his foot in midair, and motioned to me with his hand to stay where I was. Then, even as I watched, he vanished among a thin stand of hardwood saplings, as a deer, by taking three steps, can disappear against its background. For several minutes I could hear nothing but the inconsequential sounds of late afternoon in the woods. Then Billy emerged.

"Did you see them?" he asked.

"See what?"

"Deer. There were deer right out there," he said.

"Really? How many?"

"I don't know. All I saw was a doe, but there were several. She had a half-grown fawn with her that was trying to nurse, and she kept cutting him off by scissoring her leg across his head. He finally backed off, like, 'Gollee, all I wanted was a swallow.'"

"You saw that? Just now?"

"Yeah," Billy smiled.

As the sun was going behind the trees, we found one of Purvis's stands. It was about twelve feet up in a double-trunk gum, directly above a little branch. I grabbed a rung of the ladder and pulled. It was secure. "Think we ought to test it?" I asked.

Billy was squatting by the branch, looking into a clear, deep pool.

"Look here," he said. I knelt beside him. A purple gum leaf splotched with yellow floated on the pool without breaking the surface tension.

"What?" I asked.

"Crawfish."

The creature was crawling numbly along the sandy bottom; it had no more color than the water did. Billy poked a stick into the pool. "Its's going to get cold tonight, fellow." The crayfish, too chilled already to move quickly, retreated slowly to the deepest part, stirring a sediment of leafmeal that covered it in its cloud. "Maybe he'll go to bed now," Billy laughed. "It's the moon of the rutting buck." Getting to his feet, he gripped a rung and looked up at the stand. "Let's see what it looks like from up there."

I followed him up the ladder with the exhilaration of a boy climbing into a tree house. The weathered plywood seat was roomy enough for two, a concession to Purvis's long legs, but it gave a little too much beneath our weight. I perched on the edge and put my feet on the top rung. The foliage below was too thick for me to see the ground. "This ought to be a good stand when the leaves fall," Billy said. "There's a trail coming right down this branch and another one coming off that ridge. Deer are bedding in that privet by the pond. You ought to be able to kill a buck out of this stand."

I thought so, too. At that moment, in fact, as the forest floor grew dark with shadow and the evening chill touched me between my shoulder blades, it was easy to envision a parade of ghostlike forms slipping along the trail beneath the stand.

"Most people take deer for granted," Billy said, "we have so many now. They see them along the road so they buy a deer rifle and get up in a stand like this and shoot the first thing they see with horns, or sometimes whether it's got horns or not, and come back and say how easy it is. They may see a lot of deer, but they don't really watch them long enough to appreciate what it is that they are hunting."

"Deer are just targets to people like that," I said.

Billy gripped my arm. "Let's be quiet a minute."

The branches overhead made a black pattern against the white

glow of sky, but the woods below us lay in a deep twilight. I didn't
know what he was up to, but I was ready to go home. I reached
for a cigarette; Billy put his hand across mine to stop me and
pointed up the trail that ran along the branch. I could see nothing. Billy whispered, "Watch." Presently, a movement caught my
eye. Straining to see into the shadows, I perceived a form, like a
figure hidden in the pattern of a carpet. It stopped beneath an
opening in the branches, a buck, but smaller than I expected one
to be. Its rack was white as chalk against the darkness, and I could
see the dark line of hair along its spine. How could Billy have
known it was coming, I wondered; by what sensors had he dis-
cerned its presence? The line of Billy's strong brow and nose
shone in the afterglow, and his black eyes danced. Something was
happening between him and that buck that I had never seen before, a sharing that I wanted too.

The buck snorted and ran, startling me so that I nearly fell from
the stand. Billy chuckled, "He smelled where we had been. I
didn't think he would come as close as he did."

Coming down from the stand, feeling with my feet for the next
rung, I knew I would be there on opening day. I would get my
buck, and Billy, hearing the shot, would come through the woods.
Regardless of the size of the rack, he would tell me it was a fine
buck and shake my hand. Then, ceremonial as a priest, he would
dip his hand into the worthy blood and paint my cheeks and forehead. I wouldn't be able to show that face in town, of course. No
one in our church or neighborhood would even have heard of the
ritual, much less understand it. And that was too damn bad. For
a moment I wondered what virtue there was in killing a deer if no
one understood what it meant. The people in Darlington might
understand, but even to them I would look pretty silly wearing

the badge of a boy. In any case, I realized, the experience belonged to the woods. Billy was the only audience that mattered.
And I would wash my face before I got back to town.

By Thanksgiving I knew every bush, tree, and rock within
sight of that tree stand. From its high perch I monitored the
changing of leaves from one week to the next and even the quality
of light as it changed, evening by evening. But I saw no deer. I
saw chipmunks and squirrels rattling the leaves on the ground
below and flights of wood ducks squealing overhead. Once I even
glimpsed the brush of a red fox, but of worthy game not so much
as the flick of a tail. Shivering through the first hour of daylight,
longing for a ray of sun through the pines, I despaired of deer. The
buck we had seen in October seemed a phantom, quickened and
made visible by the power of Billy's imagination, or if it had been
real, an aberrant creature strayed from the routine ways of its
kind, never to come my way again. At such times Billy's rifle, a
forty-four magnum automatic, felt awkward in my hands. Having
never fired it, I had trouble believing I ever would, or that something so cold and technical could be the agent of my apotheosis as
a hunter.

A week before the season ended Billy suggested that I give up
the stand. "They're not moving in that area," he said. "I think you
ought to try something else, like the hill behind the feedlots."

That was the site of the pond where I had first shot ducks with
Purvis. "I don't think there are any stands back there," I said.

"Hunt on the ground," he said.

That meant stalking, a form of hunting that I associated with
the skill and experience of someone like Billy. But I reasoned

quickly that I could do no worse on the ground than I had in the tree. "Where are you going to hunt?" I asked.

"I have to be in Atlanta Saturday," he said.

My disappointment was too great to hide. Not only was I reluctant to go into strange woods alone before daylight, in some sense I felt betrayed, as though his letting a meeting in Atlanta take precedence over hunting divested the hunt of its purpose and importance. "I see."

Refusing to acknowledge my pout, he added, "You need to get there early. I think you're going to kill him."

Since I had not seen even a doe, I didn't share Billy's confidence. But that hardly mattered. Without his being there, I realized, I wasn't eager to kill a deer anyway. Yet I felt compelled to go because he expected me to. Maybe that uncertainty of purpose accounted for my sleeping through the alarm. I awoke that morning to broad daylight, swearing as I rolled out of bed and stumbled into my clothes. Jane, half-conscious with sleep, mumbled her surprise that I would still want to go. "Hell, yes," I said, too emphatically, vaguely irritated by her lack of understanding, angry at Billy and especially at myself for sleeping late. As I left the room she wanted to know what time I'd be getting back.

The night had brought the first hard freeze of the season; the morning was bright and clear. I parked the station wagon by a pair of silos and stepped out onto the frozen ground. The smell of silage was sweet and rank on the cold air, and the cattle were bawling in the feedlots. I had just bought a lever-action thirty-thirty. I slung it over my shoulder and reached for binoculars and possibles bag, hoping I had everything I might need but not wanting to take the time to look. A farmhand drove into the lot on a big John

Deere tractor and grinned at me. I was embarrassed to be seen arriving so late and decided to ignore him by examining the contents of my bag, but he yelled something over the clatter of the tractor, and I smiled back, a dumb, sort of helpless smile, and waved.

Crossing hardened furrows of a bean field that lay between the hill and the river, I decided to go as quickly as possible to the ridge above the pond and sit for an hour or so. Maybe I'd see a buck. As I entered the woods by a logging road, the sun was coming over the line of trees along the river, touching each bent and stiffened clump of sedge and causing it to glitter. I could smell the new oiled leather of my rifle strap. Fifty yards in front of me a doe walked across the road, from right to left toward the silos up the hill. I dropped to my knees and half-raised the rifle. A smaller doe appeared. My heart was pounding in my ears. Then two more. And suddenly he was there, his nose to the rump of the last doe—an antlered buck. Everything blurred except his head and polished rack. Through the 'scope the cross hairs wavered and jerked so that I had to lower the rifle. When I looked again he was disappearing into the brush, his head already obscured by tall grass. Though unsure of my aim, I fired. The blast filled the woods, obliterating my vision. I recovered to see white flags bounding up the hill through the pines. Getting to my feet, I released a long-held breath, a plume of vapor, and tried to calm down. After a minute I walked to the place where the deer had crossed and looked in the road for blood. A noise to my left as of some indefinite movement attracted my attention, and there he lay, wild and big in the frozen grass. He was not dead.

I had read that it's dangerous to approach a wounded buck from the front so I circled warily to his rear. His rack was not as big as

I had thought but he was, and his odor was strong. Before I knew what was happening, he was on his feet, lunging heavily up the hill. Frantic, I raised my rifle and tried to find him in the 'scope. Eighty yards away he stopped, listing to one side, and looked back toward me. His image was small in the field of view. Quartering away from me, he presented little neck and shoulder. I held as far forward on the rib cage as I could and shot again. This time I got an impression of his plunging to the right, on a course parallel to the road. I stumbled up the eroded hill and, finding the spot where he had stood, followed in the direction he had taken. After two hundred yards of growing anxiety, I found him piled up at the foot of a downed treetop. His large green eye was glazed. I prodded him on the rump with the barrel of my rifle. He didn't flinch so I grabbed an antler and hefted the head.

So it is done. I thought. *It sure wasn't a dance though. It was dumb luck.* Deciding to smoke before I faced the problem of what to do next, I sat down and lit my pipe. I looked at the deer again, lying in the leaves, its white belly shining in the sun, and noticed its hard little polished hooves. A wren was scolding from the branches of the dead treetop, and I realized that I'd never stopped hearing the tractor. I could even smell the silage. I felt an impulse to apologize and decided I'd better get busy.

I drew my knife, testing its edge with my thumb, and tried to remember the illustrated instructions I had seen in the outdoor magazines. When I knelt beside the animal, the thawing mud soaked through the knees of my one-piece outfit. I ran my fingers lightly over the belly. It was hard and distended. Hundreds of little ticks were crawling through the hair around the genitals. My knife felt as useless in my hand as a tennis racket. Billy ought to be here, I thought. He would show me what to do. Better than that, he would show me by doing it himself. *So*, I realized, *it's not just the not knowing how that's bothering you. If you can shoot an animal so easy, looks like you ought to be able to cut it open.*

I pinched the skin low in the center of the belly and made a horizontal cut, inserted the index and middle fingers of my left hand, and lifted the skin so as not to puncture the abdomen. I had no idea where things were in there. Placing the blade between my fingers, I worked carefully toward the sternum, lifting and cutting. The sound was like that of fabric tearing. The slick gut bulged forth, an obscene globe, releasing heat but no blood nor any strong foul odor.

Now what? I wondered. Whatever I was to do, I'd do it better with bare arms, so I climbed out of my camouflage and pushed the sleeves of my undershirt to my elbows. After two or three tentative slices around the confusion of organs, I said to hell with it and began slashing blindly, deep within the cavity. When I cut through the diaphragm, the hot blood bathed my hands and arms. Finally, something parted, and the whole steaming mass slid free. I stood up and pushed it aside with my foot and wiped my hands on my jeans. They were sticky and suddenly cold. I could do nothing more until I washed them. The nearest water was up the hill at the equipment shed but I didn't want to go walking into the activity of people working. I decided on the pond.

When I came over the crest of the hill, the sheet of ice below me glistened in the sun. I went down to the edge of the pond and opened a hole with my heel, then knelt and swished my knife blade clean. The water caused the fat to congeal in white caking on the blade. I wiped the blade on my jeans and dipped my arms to the elbows in the freezing, dirty pool. *This blood*, I thought, as I scrubbed them clean and rubbed the stains from my fingers.

If Billy had been there the blood would have been on my face. "Hold still," he would have said. "I don't want to get this in your beard and eyebrows." Then with his hand still wet he would have clasped mine and smiled and said, "Well done, deer slayer." I wiped my hands on my pants and held them out to the cold air, strangely white and inoffensive. I felt a little cheated, like a person who receives a degree in absentia. I would kill more deer. I was sure of that. Probably while hunting with Billy. But this moment could never come again. *He should have been here*, I thought.

Returning through the woods, I came upon the buck before I expected to. For a second it startled me, lying in the sun, an intractable fact with its tongue clamped between its teeth like a sponge. The cattle up the hill continued their anguished bawling, and that eternal wren still scolded from the downed treetop. *What do I do with it now?* I wondered. Without a sheet of plastic or even newspaper I was not prepared to take it back in the family station wagon, but that was what I would have to do. *Jane's going to love that*, I thought. I could imagine the scene in our driveway—the successful hunter home from the hill, the children standing silent, and Jane: "I hope that thing hasn't ruined the carpet."

I gathered up my gear—rifle, bag, binoculars and coveralls—and walked out to the field. It was only five minutes away, but the dragging of the buck took half an hour. Exhausted and hot, I walked up the hill to the silos to get the car. No one was there. The big green tractor was parked in the equipment shed. I rummaged around the shed and found enough old fertilizer sacks to cover the bed of the station wagon. Then I drove down the edge of the field to the place where I had left the deer. To get it into the back I had to stand on the tailgate, lifting the deer by its antlers high enough to pull the upper part of its body into the vehicle. After arranging the sacks beneath its head and leaking cavity, I folded its already stiffening legs and slammed the tailgate shut. Then I saw my reflection in the window. My forehead was smeared with red. *I'll be damned*, I thought. *That must have happened when I was cleaning the deer, scratching an itch or brushing my hair from my face.*

And suddenly I realized that Billy had stayed away on purpose. He must have decided that this was something I had to handle on my own, not only the dressing and dragging, but the being by myself with the killing for a while as well.

I got into the car and turned the rearview mirror for a better look—the spilled blood in my hand, my hand on my face, a baptism with all rights and privileges thereunto pertaining. Whether or not it would take we would have to wait and see. But something told me I shouldn't wash my face till I got home.

6
Bewildered

Anyone who spends much time in the woods is likely sooner or later to lose his bearings. Thoreau considered that a valuable experience, for not until then, he contends, "do we experience the vastness and strangeness of Nature," which may enable us to find ourselves and realize where we are. Such an epiphany as he describes might send us all in search of big woods. Yet Daniel Boone, who wandered confused for three days in the wilderness of Kentucky, claimed no such discovery, allowing only that he was "bewildered." With scantier woods these days, the Savannah River swamp was the best I could do, but that was deep enough for me to see that Boone's word should be pronounced with a long *i*.

The section of swamp I'm speaking of lay within the boundaries of a plantation on the Carolina side of the river. The name of the plantation was Groton. In 1975 a member of the family who owned it invited ten of his friends to form a hunting club there. He called it the T. Huntington Abbot Rod and Gun Club. During the first year of the club's existence the members, except for Billy Claypoole, hunted deer from tree stands on the higher, cultivated ground that people called The Hill. Only Billy hunted in the swamp. By the second year, when I joined the club, the rest of the members were beginning to discover that the swamp was not as formidable as they had thought. Sawn stumps and old roads reminded the hunter that the forest for all its majesty was not virgin, and in recent years plantation management had built a system of jeep trails for the purpose of patrolling the swamp against poachers from the river. Along with a creek called Clearwater Stream that flows south through the middle of the swamp, these lines provided boundaries for five-hundred-acre hunting sections. With the addition of a few invisible lines, the club imposed a grid upon the sunless riverbottom and made it safe. Yet we were still in awe of it. Though we could now hunt without fear of getting lost, everyone took a compass with him. When I joined the club I went to the swamp as others did, but at first I stayed close to a road or the creek. It was not until one particular November weekend that I got turned around.

I went to the swamp that morning with a big, red-faced man named Jack Bass. Though he and I were members of the same church in Athens, I had known him only from a distance, as a socially prominent building contractor, and from a newspaper photograph tacked to the church bulletin board—Jack posed like Hemingway over a fallen moose. Somewhere in Alaska. My brief time in the club had not brought us closer. Under ordinary circumstances neither of us would have chosen the other as a hunting companion; but we had drawn adjacent sections the night before, and Jack had a vehicle, and I didn't. So I arranged to ride with him.

The sky was already turning pale in the southeast as we came off the hill, and Jack was in a hurry. Maneuvering his Blazer around potholes and hog wallows with one hand and stuffing sweet rolls into his mouth with the other, he sometimes hit what he was trying to avoid, causing the headlights to swing wildly upon the trees and the aluminum tray of sweet rolls to slide across the dash from his side to mine. Turning south off the main swamp road, we bounced along a trail that ran beside Clearwater Stream. The woods on the other side were open and dark, enticing the imagination to make deer of fleeting shadows. Once we almost hit a shoat, one of the feral pigs that ranged the swamp. Jack, who was an avid pig hunter, said "Hot damn, Jim," stopped the Blazer, and reached for his short-barreled forty-four magnum. But the pig had scurried into the cane by the time he opened the door.

We came at last to a cherrybark oak that stood in a clearing by the creek. Because of its size and central location, the tree was a designated landmark. We called it the Big Oak. Jack parked the Blazer beneath it, pulling up so close to the creek that I could have seen the water if there had been enough light. One sticky roll was left in the aluminum tray. "Want that sweet roll, Jim?" Jack asked.

I said no thank you.

"Better eat it now. You don't want to go in the swamp on an empty stomach."

I said I was all right, thanks, and opened the door. Jack reached for the tray.

The morning was colder than I had dressed for. I looked up. A few stars were shining still in the deep blue dome overhead; the sun would rise in a clear sky. As I poked bullets into the magazine of my forty-four, I looked forward eagerly to the sun's warmth, still two hours away.

"How long you want to hunt?" I whispered.

"They're serving breakfast at eleven," Jack said.

"Sounds good."

"You want to set your watch with mine?"

I told Jack I didn't wear a watch but not to worry, I had learned to keep up with the hour pretty well. "What time is it right now?" I asked.

"Ten minutes till seven."

I lit a cigarette and held it up, watching the smoke. Air was stirring out of the west.

"Hope you get him," Jack said and started across the narrow wooden bridge toward his section. His huge bulk, in silhouette now against the paling swamp, was hung all about with the paraphernalia of hunting—rifle, camera, binoculars, cartridge belt, and possibles bag. I wondered how he could move quietly through the woods. He *was* a successful hunter—I had to admit that—but I was reluctant to call him good. Good-natured maybe, but lacking sensitivity, not overwhelmed enough by the beauty of the swamp. Just the day before, for example, he had told some of us a story about hunting with his eleven-year-old son, Bubba. "Anybody want to kill a pig I'll let you use Bubba. We hadn't gotten in the woods good before he said he had to do 'number two.' I said, 'Okay, but hurry up.' Directly I heard him hollering. What had happened was, he'd got all hunkered down and this little old piney-wood rooter come up right close behind him and grunted. I looked over there, old Bubba was going in five different directions. All I could see was them long skinny white legs of his and his arms waving like a windmill, trying to grab his gun with one hand and pull up his britches with the other and keep from falling over backwards in it all at the same time. And that little shoat crashing off through the brush, grunting and squealing." Jack did an imitation, laughing. "Little pig was scared as Bubba was. I told him, I said, 'Bubba, if you think you can take a crap ever' time we go hunting, I'll start bringing you along for pig bait. But, son, you got to learn not to jump like that when they grunt.'"

I couldn't help laughing at Jack, but as I watched him moving off into the dim woods I felt that his stories turned the swamp into a barnyard. Billy had said that Jack never strayed far from the road because he was too badly out of shape for a long drag. Well, he could have the trampled edges. I was going into deeper woods than he hunted. I crossed the bridge and turned south. With the wind out of the west, I would hunt the cane thickets along Clearwater Stream for a couple of hours then swing around and work my way back to the Big Oak.

The swamp is mysterious at any time or season, but in the still light of that dawn it seemed enchanted. I moved among trees spaced as widely as columns in a cathedral, obtaining with each step a new prospect down the long green aisles. I moved slowly, for it was the time of day for deer to be moving too, slipping through stands of cane or crossing open lanes as quietly as drifting smoke. I found it easier here than anywhere I'd ever been to imagine that I was in primeval forest. Yet again and again I came upon stumps, old relics of virgin forest ribbed and bleached but showing still the level cut of a crosscut saw. The stumps were cypress, but an old plantation black man named George Frazier had told us they cut hardwoods as well: "Cyperce, gum, oak and ash, tupla and sickymo."

"It taken us fours hours one day to cut down one tree," George had told us. "And dat about seven, eight foot up een de air. Little bit more dan eight. Standing on a jump board. Us start at eight o'clock dat morning to sawing and at twelve o'clock de tree hit de ground. And never stop to even get a drink of water. Mens sitting right dere looking at us. Two men. Old man Griffeth been one. Right dere sitting down looking at us."

I had asked George if they used a crosscut saw.

"Eight-foot crosscut saw. Man on each end. And after lunch us start back zackly at one o'clock, and when de man whoop for four-thirty us cut off the first cut."

How long a log?

"One stick sixteen foot. De truck didn't been but one cut high."

"Truck?" I had asked, finding it hard to imagine such a machine in this garden, gears grinding, engine revving, tires spinning in a mud hole.

"Yessuh," George Frazier had said. "Bulldog Mack."

I hunted for an hour before I discovered that I had left my compass at the cabin. I was reaching into my bag for it because I had drifted away from the creek, hunting into the wind. When my fingers failed to close on the familiar square of hard plastic, I stopped where I was, alarmed, and reached for a cigarette. For the first time I noticed that the sky had turned chalky gray; except for a blurred glimmer through the trees there was no sun. *It should be higher than that by now*, I thought, *and not in that direction. Not if the wind is holding out of the west.* The creek had to be in front of me, probably no more than two hundred yards. I started toward it, walking rapidly.

Most of the Groton swamp consists of open hardwood flats interspersed with stands of switch cane. Often the flats are long, narrow aisles walled on either side by cane thickets. From any particular spot, these aisles appear to lie in straight lines, creating an impression in the observer that he can follow them in one direction for a long way. In fact, however, they bend in subtle curves. Sometimes an aisle ends in a cane thicket. When that happens, one seeks the thinnest growth as a way through, heedless of the direction he is taking. Or sometimes his way is blocked by a deep, wide slough that local people call a "gut." Then he has to follow its twisting course in one direction or the other until he comes to a log that reaches all the way across. In these ways the physical features of the swamp can determine the path a hunter takes, especially when he has neither compass nor sun to reckon by.

When I realized I had walked far enough to have hit Clearwater Stream if it were where I had figured, I stopped and sat on a log. Two hundred yards in another direction might find it, I thought, but I would have to forget about hunting. If I killed a deer in this situation I would have a real problem, unable either to drag the carcass with me until I found my way or to leave it behind with any expectation of finding it again. I was too anxious to locate the creek anyway to concentrate on game. I smoked my last cigarette then slung my rifle over my shoulder and started in search of the creek.

I wandered through the woods for at least an hour. Once I was sure I had stumbled upon familiar ground—a low ridge where a holly stood, a fresh scrape under one of its branches. The scrape was there but the slough I expected on the other side of the ridge was not; I stood in consternation, looking out upon a gloomy cypress bottom, reluctant to cross it.

Once I found myself walking in an old logging road. Trees of good size grew in it, but its bed was sunken and easy to follow. For a hundred yards or so the expectation grew within me that the road would lead me out, and I was glad of the bulldog Macks. But as quietly as it had begun the road ceased, obliterated by leaves, and I was adrift again in the aimless woods.

Going through a thicket, I found myself deeper in taller and denser cane than I had ever been. Hogs came to mind, the danger of stumbling upon a rutting boar or a sow with a litter of pigs. I took my rifle from my shoulder and held it before me, shielding my face from the whipping cane. The thicket went on and on. I felt claustrophobic, unable to see, hot and unable to breathe. Leading with my shoulder, I plunged through the woven stalks, scratched my eye on a twig, and tripped. On all fours I emerged abruptly from the cane, as through a solid wall. And almost tumbled down a bank into a deep, dry slough.

Pigs had recently passed that way. Like a harrow they had turned the soft, black dirt. Using a cypress knee for a foothold I descended into the slough. The ground was strewn with tupelo fruit. Dark as a plum and speckled, it looks like something good to eat, abundant mast for wild animals, but it is too bitter, they say, even for pigs, and it bleeds a thin red juice. Once when I was looking for a wounded deer, the stain of that juice on a leaf had fooled me into thinking I was on the track of the animal.

Seeking firm footing to cross the slough, I discovered, half-buried in the mud, a bridge of logs laid snugly side by side. *A corduroy ford*, I realized. *The logging road again. Maybe it picks up on the other side.* But where the road should have cut the bank I found tracks, some person's bootprints, clear impressions an inch or so deep in the soft dirt of the edge. Startled at first by a feeling that someone had encroached upon my section, I was even more startled to realize that the tracks of course were my own and that I had no recollection of having passed that way. How could I have failed to recognize the place? And how could I have failed to notice, the first time by, the old log ford? The tracks came within a few feet of it. I sat down on a log, feeling a little sorry for the one who made them. They looked so confident, so sure they knew where they were going, continuing in a straight line down the edge of the slough. Yet here we were. The dismal light reduced the world to a monochrome, tree trunks no different in tone from the wet hanks of Spanish moss that hung above my head, the dim, distant curtain of wood hardly darker than the sky. I wanted a cigarette. I wanted the hell out.

This is no virgin Kentucky wilderness, I reminded myself, but only a narrow ribbon of woods along the Savannah River. Ten men were hunting within a few miles of me—Jack within a few hundred yards—and the cabin itself was less than a mile away. By walking for an hour in a straight line I would come out on one road or another, or at worst the river. The problem was to keep a straight line without a compass.

George Frazier had told me of two black men named Reuben and Steven who had lived on the plantation back in the twenties and thirties. Even now, forty years after the last one died, George referred to them as the "swamp men." They had lived in cabins on the hill and planted a little cotton, but mostly they had ranged the swamp, at any season, for three or four days at a time, to hunt along the river. "Didn't need no roads," George had said. "Didn't wear no watch." Striking out in opposite directions at daybreak, they would agree to meet at a certain tree in the middle of the afternoon, and sure enough they would both show up, emerging at about the same time from the flat, dim woods.

"They just knew the swamp that well?" I had asked.

"Born to it, suh," George had said. "Just born to it."

I thought of Reuben and Steven as I sat on the log, saw them easing through the green sameness of the swamp, mile after mile, up and down the river. How long would it take to learn the swamp that well, I wondered, or rather, *what* would it take? For their knowledge of the swamp was not mere familiarity with the location of particular trees and sloughs, it was attitude, achieved in part by indifference to watch and compass, in part by adjustment to the inevitability of here and now. Such a person could no more get lost than a deer can, I realized, for wherever he finds himself is all right with him. What blessed freedom. George Frazier was right: you had to be born to it. *The fact that I am lost must mean that I'm a watch-and-compass man.*

I wondered what time it was. I usually kept track on cloudy days by consciously noting the lapsing of thirty-minute segments, but I had been so distracted this morning by trying to get unlost that I now had no more idea of the hour than I did of my location. I was probably within earshot of the horn of Jack's Blazer, but the prospect of being found by the honk of a vehicle got me to my feet. I decided to backtrack myself as far as my bootprints would take me.

They took me back up the slough to a deer crossing where I had come down into it. But on the firm higher ground, I stood in an utterly strange place, convinced I had never been there before. I wondered if I would be able to hear Jack's horn.

I heard instead the squeal of wood ducks, not the contented whistlings of feeding ducks but their shrill alarm cry, accompanied by a sound of splashing, and almost immediately three ducks wheeled above me, flared and swung away through the trees. *Something flushed those ducks,* I thought. *And it wasn't me.* I took the rifle from my shoulder and dropped to my knees. *Pigs maybe. Or a bobcat.* I had no intention of shooting a cat, of course, and I didn't want to shoot a pig, but I was prepared for game, suddenly a cat myself, crouched and ready to spring.

The ducks had flushed from a place on the slough above me. I approached on hands and knees, lifted my head, and peeped over the edge. There was an otter. Half-submerged in shallow water, it was sleek and dark and bigger than I had thought one could grow, and its whiskered snout was as blunt as the end of a log. It was busy with something it held in its paws. I raised my binoculars for a better look. What it was holding was neither frog nor fish but a chunk of meat, red and as round as a softball. Securing it with its paws against a thick root that twisted like an otter itself from the bank into the slough, the animal tore off a piece, lifted his head straight up and gulped it down. Then he lowered his head and tore at the chunk again. The otter's casual ferocity was exciting. I had never witnessed such a plain fact. I could almost taste the meat myself. Suddenly I knew what it was, could all but see the unsuspecting duck, its wings suddenly, terribly slapping the surface, then the slow roll of muddy water and then, popping up, the blunt head, jaws stuffed. I felt the feathery convulsions in my own mouth and clamped my jaws for a better grip.

Brutal jaws.

A shot rang out, not far away. The otter flowed over the root and disappeared, leaving its meal, and I remembered I was lost.

I got to my feet, a little disoriented. I could course the shot and reckoned that I should. It had to be Jack.

Another stretch of old logging road led me straight into the area from which the shot had come. Not finding Jack, I stopped every fifty yards or so to listen for sounds of dragging. I didn't want to call out, but I was beginning to think I might have to. Coming upon an open aisle, I stopped and swept the far reaches with my binoculars.

"You not lost are you, Jim?"

I jumped. The voice was close. On my right. And there he was, his face dark red and streaming. A good-sized hog lay at his feet with a rope strung through cuts between the tendons and bones of its hind legs.

"Sonofabitch, Jack. You scared me. No. I just heard you shoot and thought you might need some help dragging."

"Well, that's good 'cause you looked like you was lost."

I sat on the log beside him and looked at the pig. It was a sow. Jack had not field-dressed it. "You got a cigarette?"

He gave me one and lit one himself.

"I guess I *was* sort of turned around," I said. "Till I heard you shoot. I left my compass at the cabin."

Jack laughed.

"You ever been lost in here?"

"Back in October. I thought you knew about that?"

"I wasn't here in October, Jack."

"That's right. You went to that wildlife art thing in Atlanta. Hell yeah I got lost. Right over there in J where you were just now. Too damn hungover that morning to remember I'd taken my compass out of my bag the day before. It ain't much fun, 'specially down here, but I got to thinking about it later; I realized there's something about this swamp that maybe you can't understand unless you do get lost in it. I don't know how to explain it, but as long as you're going by a compass it's like you're still in town or something. But without one it's like you aren't really in any one certain place exactly. I started noticing stuff I'd never looked at before— that orange fungus that looks like sea shells on the side of a log, owls, stuff like that. What do you call those big old owls?"

"Barred owls."

"I was sitting there trying to catch my breath, one of them suckers flew into a tree over my head and hooted. God-almighty.

That's the wildest damn thing I ever heard. This might sound funny to you, but I sort of felt like hooting back."

"I know," I said. "I saw this ot—"

"I almost forgot I was lost there for a minute."

"That's exactly—"

"Let me ask you something, Jim. If a person doesn't know he's lost—I mean, if he forgets he's lost or doesn't care whether he is or not—can you really say he *is* lost? You know what I'm trying to say?"

"Yes," I said, amazed, and thought, *Where you'd be then is wild. With a fast grip on the here and now and a strong appetite for it.*

Jack was getting to his feet, but I was on to something: *Reuben and Steven were like that otter, but there was nothing blessed or even free about the way that thing tore that chunk of meat. So how could you say—?*

"What did you see?" Jack asked.

"An otter. It was the damndest thing, Jack. It was like what you were saying—"

"Well, that's good. But if you want to get back in time for breakfast you better give me a hand with Miss Piggy here."

I looked at the sow. "They drag a lot easier if you field-dress them first," I said.

"They drag like a sack of cement whether you field-dress them or not. But we ain't got far to go. We're right at the Big Oak."

"*Really?*" I said, and looked in the direction Jack had indicated. Through the thick foliage I could see the blaze of his orange vehicle.

I

A FRIEND OF MINE SAID to a group of our university colleagues one day, "Jim goes hunting so he can come back and tell us about it." I was annoyed by his smugness, but later, after giving the matter some thought, I realized he was on to something. The telling *is* important—not a primary reason, perhaps, but for many of the hunters I have known it's a necessary conclusion to the killing of game.

If I disliked anything about killing my first buck, it was having no one to tell the story to. All the way back to Athens I rehearsed the sequence of events that ended with the deer on the ground, wondering all the way who my audience might be. My eight-year-old son John would listen gladly, but Billy was out of town, and Jane, I knew, would not want to hear it. I had been wrong in guessing that her reaction would be to complain about the odor and the blood; what she actually did when she saw the dead wild animal in the back of the station wagon was feel sorry for it, *poor thing*. As I drove through the streets of my subdivision, men were working in every yard, husbands in shirt sleeves, raking leaves, and I grew depressed.

There is an Eskimo folktale in which an eagle goddess threatens a young hunter with death unless he agrees to learn what she calls the songfeast—a posthunt celebration in which the hunter reenacts the chase and distributes meat and furs to the guests.

When I joined the T. Huntington Abbot Club at Groton, I found that the members held a songfeast every night. It would begin quietly as hunters came in from the field at dark—so quietly that if you were new in the club or a guest you wouldn't realize until later that anything had started at all. It might begin with one man saying to another, standing at the bloody tailgate of a pickup truck, "Well. Tell me about it."

The other man might say, "Let me get something to drink first."

Out of the dark someone else would speak. "What do you want? You want a beer? I got a Coors."

With the pop of the can, the telling would start—usually with a standard introduction, "There's really not that much to tell," though Billy Claypoole almost always began his stories by saying, "It was a really good hunt."

The coming in of hunters from the field would continue for an hour after dark, each arrival a minor event met by the curiosity of flashlight beams probing the bed of the truck: "Where is he?" someone would ask. "I heard you shoot." If the beams of light struck horn and hair, someone would say, "All *right*," or "God-amighty" if the antlers were a heavy, curving rack: "Y'all come looka here." Most of the time of course they weren't. Often the deer was a doe; or if it were a buck, a spike or a three-point. Then the men in camp would offer a perfunctory congratulation: "That's good. Glad you got him." As small groups began to move into the cabin, someone would remember his manners and ask the successful hunter what stand he'd been hunting from.

A table in front of the fire offered a variety of appetizers, usually crackers, cheese, and dip but sometimes shrimp or oysters on the half-shell and rarely some special fare, like stone crabs or smoked salmon. Amidst the coming and going, the putting away of gear and pouring of drinks, men would gather around the food, and the hunter would have a chance to elaborate. "I was in the Thin Air Stand," he'd say.

"See many deer?"

"About fourteen. But I couldn't get a shot at anything until I saw that spike."

"Were they crossing through that broomsedge off to the right? Along that ditch?"

"Every one of them. From five-thirty on, it was a damn parade going through."

"Any bucks?"

"I couldn't tell. In all that brush. That little spike was the only buck I saw that I know of, and he came out by himself. Just stepped right out into that plowed field on the left as you're looking toward the swamp. It was getting so late by then I don't think I would have seen him if I hadn't just happened to be looking in that direction."

"I *thought* I heard somebody shoot late. How long a shot was it?"

"I stepped off a hundred and twenty paces from the tree."

"Damn. Good shot. Hit him in the neck too."

The hunter would look around, smiling at the men who were listening. "I didn't want him to run off. With it getting dark and all."

A big buck required more of a story than that, and the story commanded a larger audience. Handled properly, the telling could last all evening, advancing in stages from the yard to the supper table to the circle around the fire. I arrived at the cabin from Athens one day to hear that Billy had killed a ten-point buck in the swamp that morning. He had just taken it to the cooler. I went out on a tree stand before he returned so I didn't see him until I came in at dark. He was standing in the yard talking to two or three others when I walked up.

"Down in D," he was saying, "right on Clearwater Stream."

"What were you doing?" someone asked. "Were you sitting down?"

"Yeah. Sort of easing along," Billy answered.

"He just step out in front of you, or what?"

"Yeah, more or less."

It was more, of course, a great deal more, but Billy was saving the story for the right audience, for the flicker of firelight and the comfort of a glass of sour-mash whiskey.

He had his audience at supper, fifteen men in camouflage seated at a long pine table on the screened porch, but the table was dominated by Jack Bass, whose wit could produce such fits of mirth that people had trouble eating. Once when the cooks served a dubious-looking casserole, Jack started it down the table with the question "Have y'all ever eat any ground-buzzard?" which was his name for a possum. Again, when someone expressed surprise that Jack liked chitlins, he said, "I could eat one from here to Estill." It was hard for Billy to tell his kind of story under those conditions, but when the plates were scraped clean and even the huge serving bowls stood empty, someone said, "We need to hear about that buck, William." Billy offered a protest, but several people said, "Tell it," so he began. "There's really not that much to tell. I was hunting a thicket on Clearwater Stream, sort of watching a crossing on the creek there; I looked back behind me once and saw this buck sneaking off, moving upstream. I could tell he had already seen me, but I was out of position so I just had to turn and shoot"—Billy spun slowly in the act of shooting, smiling—"in one fluid motion."

The table erupted in laughter. A doctor who had had too much to drink said, "We don't need to hear none of this one-fluid-motion shit. Heh. Heh. Everybody knows you're a damn Indian. We gonna have to change your name, call you old One-Fluid-Motion Claypoole. Ain't that what the Indians did? Heh. Heh."

That stopped the telling, but Billy had finished the supper-table version anyway. If he had been engaged in the unabridged edition, his lips might have tightened at the doctor's interruption and his eyes darkened, for he expected a serious story to be taken seriously. As it was, he had asked for the response he got, and now he was laughing too.

The movement of men from the table on the porch to the fireplace in the cabin often took as long as thirty minutes, as people planned the next day's hunt, swapping the sections they had drawn and arranging for rides to the swamp. I found a seat in the circle around the hearth and settled in, waiting for Billy. I wanted to hear the whole story, enacted before an audience of men who understood and cared, and I knew that Billy wanted to tell it. Not for the sake of his own glory, but in tribute to the deer. Whether an animal was big or little, easy or difficult, if it were slain, Billy felt, it deserved the honor of a story, even when the telling might reveal some failure on the part of the hunter. He had been critical more than once of people who refused to share the details of a successful hunt. Of one man who kept silent about killing a button buck, Billy said, "It's like he buried it in the woods."

I wished that he would come on. If he did not get started before Jack Bass came in, he would never get to tell it, not to this group of men, because once Jack established himself in front of the fire all talk of hunting would cease. Just now Jack was busy at the bar, emptying what was left of a fifth of Ancient Age into an iced-tea tumbler. This was Billy's chance, and sure enough he stepped from the shadowed room into the circle of firelight and backed up to the hearth. I said, "All right. I want to hear more about that buck, Billy." He turned and spat into the fire. Then, turning back to us, he smiled: "It was a really beautiful hunt."

Above the mantel behind him the mounted head of a buck presided over the room, the faltering light of a gas lantern dancing in its glassy eyes. "I was easing through some pretty thick cane along the creek, and I just started feeling like a buck was in there somewhere."

People were always asking Billy questions about technique, hoping to discover in his answers the secret of his consistent success. In the statement he had just made he had revealed the secret as fully as he ever would, and no one as far as I could tell had even noticed. Probably because they were expecting the kind of explanation you find in the outdoor magazines: "Surefire Tips for a Trophy Buck." And Billy's secret could not be explained: "I just started feeling like a buck was in there somewhere."

I couldn't account for it myself, and I had seen it happen, one day not long before, when he and I were easing through a thicket in the swamp. I had just killed a spike, out near the river, and Billy, hunting in an adjacent section, had come to the sound of the shot. We had field-dressed the deer and hidden the carcass under a brushpile so the buzzards wouldn't find it, and then we had started across the swamp toward Billy's Blazer, to bring it around to a point closer to the kill. I was relaxed, casual, and talking freely. Billy stopped me. "Let's hunt this thicket up here, Jim." I could tell by the way he was holding his body and the tone and pitch of his voice that he was already on to the presence of game.

The cane grew thin enough for us to walk through it without brushing the stalks with our shoulders. We were walking abreast, never more than fifteen yards apart, but I had to keep an eye on him because his soft, old, faded clothes blended with the colors and textures of the swamp. At some point I looked away for a moment and when I turned toward him again he had disappeared. I stopped, amazed, and listened for the sound of his feet. After an uncertain minute or two, I gave a low whistle. And there he was, standing in the spot where I had last seen him, his finger emphatically to his lips. I felt silly, embarrassed. He pointed slowly to the cane in front of us and with a downward motion of his hand signaled me to stay put. Then with two steps he vanished again. I don't know how long I stood there; it seemed like ten minutes. when he appeared next, he was at my side, unannounced by any rustling of leaves. He wanted to know if I had seen the buck. I had to confess that I had not seen anything. A buck had been between us, he said, just before I whistled.

Between us? In that thin cane. "Really?"

"He sneaked out ahead of us. I just caught a glimpse of him for a second, just about the time you whistled. He was flat-out on his belly."

It was a wonder to me that the buck had escaped detection, evaded, avoided, eluded, on such bare ground, but no less wonderful was Billy's achievement of the same invisibility. It was only my detection of course that they escaped, not each other's, for Billy had spied the buck when I had not and the buck had seen him when I had no idea where he was. I felt dense with self-con-sciousness, as obvious as an old chimney in an open field.

Now, standing in front of the fire, Billy was saying, "The cane was so thick I couldn't see five feet in front of me, but when I stopped I could hear a deer walking—*crunch, crunch, crunch*—real slow, off to my right, like he was trying to sneak away. When he stopped, I tried to move on him, but he kept slipping away."

One of the guests in camp interrupted. "How did you know it was a buck?"

"He was sort of acting like a buck," Billy said. "Finally, I lost track of him, but I knew he was still in the thicket."

"How?" the guest asked.

"What?"

"How could you tell he was still in there?"

Billy smiled, knowing his answer would sound like magic. "I just had this feeling. I knew he was trying to move west toward those big thickets in D . . . "

I wondered how he had known that.

" . . . so I eased over to the creek where I could watch this crossing below me. I figured it was just a matter of time before he stepped out. Now this is the beautiful part, y'all. While I was watching the crossing, I noticed a flock of turkeys on the other side of the creek, sort of drifting out of a thicket into an oak flat there. It was really—"

"Turkeys?" the guest asked. "You saw turkeys?"

"Hens and poults. Yeah. They were really neat. One little gob-bler kept feeding out ahead of everybody else just like a ten-year-old trying to impress his little sisters, and those hens were fussing at him like a couple of old schoolteachers. I was enjoying the turkeys so much I had almost forgotten the buck when all of a sudden one of the hens putted"—Billy did a perfect imitation of the turkey's alarm note—"and everybody got nervous and started clucking. I knew they couldn't have seen me so they had to be reacting to something behind me. I just eased my whole body around real slow trying to get in position to shoot—"

"You knew it was the buck?" the guest asked.

"He must have just that second stepped out of the cane toward the creek and saw me at the same instant the turkeys saw him. He had his neck stretched out low in front like he knew he had too much rack and no place to hide it, and, I swear, he was tiptoeing."

"And that's when you went into your one-fluid-motion act?" someone else asked.

"It was beautiful. He had me totally faked out. He would have made it too if it hadn't been for those turkeys."

People in the group began to stir; some moved toward the bar, others congratulated Billy on his hunt. A man named Charlie Creedmore said, "Hey, y'all wait a minute. Billy's leaving out the best part. Tell them about the canoe, Billy."

"Why don't you tell them, Charlie," Billy said. "My glass is empty."

Charlie was already a little drunk, but he managed to get to his feet. "Me and Bill Willett were walking up Main Swamp Road, coming in from G, and just as we got to the bridge, here comes Claypoole, right down Clearwater Stream, in a damn canoe. It was like something you'd see in a movie—Billy floating around the bend, sort of parting the Spanish moss, and this humongous damn buck hanging all over the front. All you could see at first was just deer and horns and then Claypoole. I wish y'all could have seen it."

Jack Bass stepped into the light and stood at the fire by Charlie. His guitar rested almost flat upon the bulge of his belly. He placed his glass on the mantel behind him and plucked a chord. "Glad you had such a great hunt, William. What I want to know is how you got that buck to wait for you right there where you left your canoe?"

Billy, lost already in the darkness of the large room, did not answer, but laughing Jack had not expected him to.

Someone asked Jack to tell the joke about the stewardess who was afraid of flying, but Jack, intent on tuning his instrument, ignored the request. Directly he stopped, took a swallow from his tumbler on the mantel, then turned his red face, already shiny with sweat, to his audience. "I ever tell·y'all about a old boy worked for us named Parshal Oats?"

"Parshal was foreman on Billups Hall—that big dorm at the top of Lumpkin Street. We just barely did get that sucker finished in time for fall quarter. Late that Friday before the students were supposed to be coming in on Sunday we did the final inspection, and damn if we didn't find two dozen mattresses that hadn't been sewed up on one side. I said, 'Sonofabitch, Parshal. We ain't got time to order new ones and get them here by Sunday.' Old Parshal said, 'Don't you worry about it, Mr. Bass. My wife can stitch them things up in no time.' She worked second shift in the sewing room at the mill. Parshal said he'd bring her over there when she got off that night. Well, she took care of it just like he said. When he came in on Monday I asked him how long it took her. She must have been up there all night, and I wanted to give her a little something for her trouble. Parshal said, 'You don't need to pay her nothing, Mr. Bass. I just thrown her down and paid her off right there.' "

Jack took out a red bandanna and wiped his streaming face while the room rocked with laughter. Before the laughs subsided, he was picking out the chords of a familiar tune. As I made my way through the dark hallway toward the bunkhouse, I could hear his rich red-clay tenor, riding the high notes, higher than I had thought he could go:

> And the beasts of the wild
> Will be led by a child
> And there will be peace,
> Peace in the valley,
> For me.

Billy was already asleep, or pretending to be.

"You awake?"

No response.

My bunk was next to his. I stepped out of my trousers, dreading the cold synthetic fabric of the sleeping bag along my bare legs. Once inside, I scrunched down and pulled the flap over my head. When I stopped shivering, I could hear Billy's breathing, peaceful and deep. I lay awake for a long time listening to him sleep. Now and then a faint burst of laughter reached me from the cabin.

Billy was fond of saying that it's not the size of the rack that matters, it's the quality of the hunt. I figured it was easier to believe that if you killed big deer from time to time. But I had never been asked to stand in front of the fire and tell about a hunt. Or ever even seen a buck as big as the one Billy had killed. I tried to imagine what one would look like in the woods, but all I could manage was that buck in the bow of Billy's canoe, its antlered head hanging over the gunwale. I seemed to be standing shoulder-deep in the parting stream and Billy was paddling straight toward me, in slow motion, and every time he shifted his weight for a paddle stroke the antlered head clattered against the side of the canoe.

II

One year later.

Midnight, and Jack Bass was still going strong. From where I sat on the bunkhouse steps I could not make out his words, but I knew by the pitch of that red-clay voice and the frequent surges of laughter from the group that Jack was still in front of the fire. I was cold but I would rather have gone to bed than join them. Not that I was angry. I was just in no mood for laughter.

I had been left in the swamp that evening and had to walk all the way in from the river. Nobody's fault, but it was still five miles, the last hour of it in the dark, and I was exhausted. What had kept me going after the day I had had was knowing that Billy would be at the cabin when I got there. He hadn't been. And now, thinking of bed, I was ready to give up. *Told me at the first of the week that he would be at Groton for supper Friday night. To hell with him if he can't ever be where he says he's going to be.* The trouble was I didn't know how I was going to get to sleep without telling him what had happened.

It was not the kind of thing I could tell the others. Any of them. And I was not sure why. They already knew the plain facts. Jack had seen to that, not in malice but because from his point of view the story was too good not to tell—sad as hell, but as deer-hunting stories go, damned good, and since he had been in on the last act, he figured it was partly his. I had managed to get through supper by shaking my head at the questions and muttering evasive answers, but I was afraid to say more, to tell the story myself, because I didn't know how it might come out. With Billy that didn't matter.

At the sound of a truck I got to my feet and walked out far enough to see. And there were headlights, small in the distance, creeping slowly across the dam. The truck came on around and turned into the Pole Bridge yard. It was Billy who stepped out. Showing his strong, even white teeth in the dark.

"It's about damn time." I tried for a bantering tone, but my voice took on an edge that I regretted. He ignored it.

"All right. How big is he?" Laughter in his voice. He was in a good mood, grabbing bags from the back of the truck.

I stepped forward, "Let me help you with those."

"You kill anything, sure enough?"

"Pig."

"*All right*. Fantastic!" Really laughing now—not because it was unusual for a pig to be killed but because I was the one who had killed it. I, who made no secret of my contempt for the mean, stupid eye of feral stock, had finally condescended to shoot a Poland China, or a Duroc or a Hampshire, or some admixture thereof, and Billy was delighted.

"No. Not fantastic. Just the bad end of a sad day."

"Is this going to take long, Kilgo, because if it is you better save it till tomorrow. I haven't slept in forty-eight hours. I got to get to bed."

"Grab a beer out of that cooler and sit down. I'll be through by the time you finish it."

He pulled two cans from the icy water, handed one to me and took a seat on the top step. I was too cold to enjoy a beer, but I saw that I had no choice. Just then a barred owl broke out somewhere between the cabin and the swamp, a loud, abandoned hooting, as lunatic as any natural sound in this part of the country. Another answered off to the south and then a third from far out in the swamp.

Billy said he loved it.

"You know how you go into B off Stephens Road? There's sort of a land bridge between those two big cypress ponds?"

"Yeah."

"You know the beaver dam on that slough that connects the ponds? Well, if you bear to the left instead of crossing the dam you come to a right thick wall of cane, and just on the other side of that cane was where I was hunting."

"Did you come out on a long oak flat that runs back toward Stephens Road?"

"That's exactly where I was. You must have hunted in there."

"It's a good place."

"Listen. There's a big cherrybark oak as soon as you come out of the cane. That's a real good place to sit. With that east pond right across the flat anything moving north and south has to pass within range of you. I hadn't been there five minutes when I saw something moving along the edge of the pond. It was still real early, and the sun was hitting the mist coming off the water. What I saw was a hog, but coming through that mist it looked like some old Pleistocene mammal, big and black, half of him head."

"How long a shot was it?"

"That's not the pig I shot."

"Oh no, Jim. Why not?" There was a shade of reproach in his voice.

"I didn't want to shoot a pig. It would have taken me the rest of the morning to drag him out—the damn thing must have weighed two hundred and fifty pounds—anyway I was hunting deer. That place felt so much like deer I was expecting a buck to materialize any second. You know how you can feel it sometimes? The only problem was that when he did, he was right behind me. He must have come out of that cane, which is the one place I didn't expect him since I had just come through there myself."

"Acting like a buck."

"Billy, he was the biggest buck I've ever seen. I don't know how I knew he was there. Maybe I heard a twig or something. Anyway, I eased my head around and he was *right there*. I couldn't have been more startled if a circus pony had come walking up. I guess it was the nearness. I mean, I could have almost stroked his side. There was no way I could shoot. My whole body was turned away from him; my rifle was the wrong way too, like this. But the funny thing, Billy, it didn't matter. At that moment it really didn't. I can't explain it. It was so . . . well, intimate is the only word I can call it. I can't explain it."

"I know."

"But, Billy, he had a tremendous rack. It was dark and heavy at the base, and I could see all those little knobby gnurls, and the tines were real high and looked like polished ivory.

"He took two steps forward, not toward me but not away from me either, and stopped with his head behind this little forked tree. I didn't think he could see me so I brought my rifle around about three-quarters, and then I saw that his head was *between* the forks and he was looking straight at me.

"I froze and he did a complete turnaround; then he took two or three steps. It happened so fast. I had an impression of that large, wild eye passing in front of me, and then he just stopped and stood still, and I had him in the scope, just a blur of hair, and I knew he was mine. It began to feel like it was ordained or something. I know this sounds strange, but I had the feeling he was being given to me.

"When I shot he leapt straight up and turned completely around, almost like he was dancing against the sun in the blast of the rifle, and then he was gone."

Billy groaned, softly. "You couldn't get off another shot?"

"I had a glimpse of him barreling away through the trees, sort of listing to one side, and that was it. I kept telling myself, *Don't panic. Just sit down and smoke a cigarette. He's not going far.* But that didn't work. I knew I'd made a bad shot. I didn't even want to go over and look for blood because I was afraid I wouldn't find any."

I paused for a swallow of beer.

"Did you?" Billy asked.

"No. But I found some hair. Just a pinch. It was white."

"Sounds like brisket."

"I know it. That's what I thought too. That's the sickest feeling I've ever had. I didn't see any way I could have missed that deer. Not at that range. Still don't. Anyway, I started out after him, and in about a hundred yards I found blood. Once he started he really painted the ground. For the next fifty yards it looked like somebody had sloshed a bucket of red all over the leaves.

"You know that strange feeling you get when you're following a blood trail? You feel sick because you've made a bad shot and you think you've lost the deer, but on the other hand the blood proves that the deer has actually been at that very spot. I mean, it's like you can't believe the buck was really true, but the blood is definitely true. The way it's spattered on the leaves. And you're thinking that no matter where he goes he's leaking this vitality and all you have to do is follow it far enough and there he'll be. I was so confident for a while there that I kept looking up, expecting every second to see him, to see his white belly shining in the sun, and then the blood began to run out and I started getting scared.

"He had run down that open flat maybe three hundred yards, then swung hard toward the river through an opening in the cane. The trail was still fairly easy to follow there where he turned to the west, so I stopped and smoked a cigarette. Told myself not to push him and get his adrenalin pumping again, but I guess I really wanted the comfort of the blood while it was still strong.

"Beyond that point it just stopped. I mean, like all of a sudden. I spent thirty minutes on my hands and knees. Finally found one little drop a good hundred yards from the last blood and it was no more than a daub, like a smear of lipstick on a leaf. I could tell from where it was that the buck had gone into a thicket, so I followed him in and came on an opening, like a little room in the cane. Soon as I stepped into it I saw a wet place in the leaves. I knelt and touched it and my fingertips came away red. The ground was soaked, Billy, the leaves all matted together. I figured he must have stood there until he saw me coming. But that was it. I never found another sign of him—no blood, no tracks, nothing."

"He had probably been lying down," Billy said. "A wound like that would get all plastered with leaves and dirt, which is why it didn't bleed anymore. You looked real good? All around?"

"The whole damned day."

"How far was that from where you shot him?"

"Couldn't have been more than four hundred yards."

"He could have covered that before you lit your first cigarette. If he went down that quickly I'd say he was hit pretty bad. Sounds to me like you pushed him too hard, Jim."

"I know. I kept telling myself to be patient, but I just couldn't wait. The whole thing was a bad case of buck fever, I guess. When that buck turned around and stopped, right in front of me, I just knew I had him, and I couldn't believe it. I could see that rack in the back of the truck and everybody coming out to admire it and asking me to tell about the hunt, and I just lost it. I was scared to death he was going to bolt any second—I could see him gathering himself—and I couldn't stand the thought of losing him. It was like somebody was handing me something I wanted more than anything else in the world and all I had to do was not drop it."

I stood up. "Anyway. That's the story."

"What about the pig?"

"Oh. Yeah. Well, I thought you'd be in by then so I decided to go back to the Pole Bridge and get something to eat, thinking maybe we could go back to the swamp in the afternoon and look some more. But when I got to Stephens Meadow, Charlie was sitting there in Jack's Blazer, and while I was telling him about it Jack came out of C. I was really surprised at how sympathetic they were, Billy. I guess they thought I was going to start crying or something. I probably was. They wanted to go back down there right then. So that's what we did. All the way down Stephens Road Jack kept saying 'Don't worry about it, Jim. We'll find your

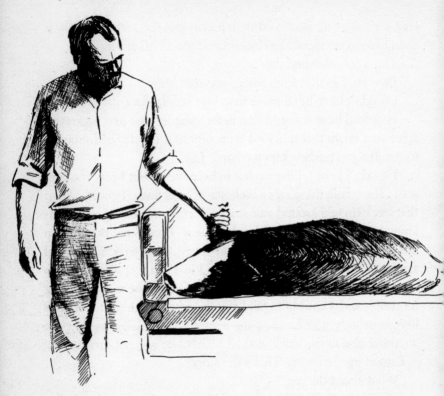

deer. He's dead as a hammer right now, I guarantee you. You just show me the last place you found blood.'

"Anyway, I killed the pig when we got back down there. They were making a wide circle toward the river, and I decided to stomp through that thicket where the buck had bedded down. I went in the back side, and almost immediately something flushed right at my feet, lunging and crashing through the cane. At first I was sure it was the buck, but it sounded too thick for a deer. Then it stopped. I brought my rifle up and the scope fell on something squat and black, and I shot without thinking. It was a sow."

"It's good you got meat," Billy said.

"Well. I guess so. But after I dragged it out of the cane and was sitting there waiting for Jack and Charlie to come up, I looked at those ugly little eyes and the dried mud caked in its bristles and thought what a different thing from a deer a pig is."

When I said that something wrenched free and began rising to the surface. For a moment I was afraid that it was going to come out in words, as inevitable as a belch, but I clamped my jaw and swallowed hard. Then I said, "Billy, I missed that buck because I was trying to snatch something."

"How much did the sow weigh?" he asked.

I wondered if he had heard me. "I don't know. A hundred and fifty pounds. Felt like three hundred by the time we got her to the truck."

"Dragging a pig is good therapy."

"I had help with that, a lot of help, as a matter of fact. Jack and Charlie probably did more dragging than I did. It was getting warm by then, and Jack was all red in the face and sweating like a pig himself. He said a deer's slick and lays close to the ground, but a 'paig' tends to plow the ground like a sack of cee-ment. I think Charlie was getting a little worried about Jack because Jack really was blowing hard. Charlie wouldn't let Jack relieve him when it came his turn to drag. When we finally got the pig out to the road, Jack put his heavy old arm around my shoulder and said, 'Jim, it's a hell of a lot harder to drag somebody else's "paig" than it is your own.' I told him yeah, I remembered. I helped him drag one my first year in the club. I wanted him and Charlie to have this one, but Jack said no, it was the Lord's will for me to shoot that pig, a consolation prize for losing the buck. He lost one like that himself last year, you remember, and he said he knew how I felt. He even wanted to go back to the swamp after we ate lunch and look some more. I was going anyway, but I hated for them to give up their whole day of hunting on my account, but Jack just said, 'Naw, Jim. You don't need to be down there by yourself. You might get depressed.' But he made me promise not to shoot another 'paig.' "

I emptied onto the ground what was left of the beer. "Bill Willett and some of them came down there later, and we got all scattered out along the river. I was by myself, and when I got back to where we had parked, everybody was gone. Everybody figuring I had gotten a ride with somebody else, I guess."

Billy placed his big blunt-fingered hand on the back of my neck, and warmth as from a campfire spread through my shoulders and along my arms.

"So that's why I walked all the way back from Matthew's Bluff. And I'm beat all to hell and want to go to bed and I sure am glad you're here, because I think maybe I can get to sleep now."

8
Grandfather

I can only apologize to this ancestral ghost for this effort at understanding. Who can read the thoughts of the dead . . . ?

Andrew Lytle, *A Wake for the Living*

I BEGAN TO UNDERSTAND the authority of family tradition when I noticed that the boys in Darlington who liked to hunt and fish were sons of men who did. As I have said, my father was one of those men. And he was because his father had been. The gun to which I was born, the sweet little L. C. Smith, was there of course before I was, in the possession and use of the Jim Kilgo for whom I was named. Then, before I was strong enough to pick it up, it was standing in the closet of my parents' room, mine but in trust only, exactly like the five hundred dollars he had deposited in my name at the savings and loan. Although I could no more touch it than I could the money, it was an imperative from the hallowed past, so heavy that the alternative of my not using it never occurred to me.

When I was able to lift it to my shoulder, my father took me hunting. We went to the farm where his father had taken him at the same age, stopping to ask permission of the widow who owned the place. As we pulled into her drive, he told me, "My daddy had standing permission to hunt out here, but he never failed to stop and tell Mrs. Law." The widow came to the door, a white-haired country woman behind the screen, drying her hands on her apron. "My, my," she said, "seems like it was just yesterday when Mr. Kilgo was bringing you out here." My father said, "Yes, ma'am," and she told him how much she appreciated his stopping at the house, and she sure did hope we'd find some birds. That kind of thing made an impression on me, as did his respect for her property, his careful attention to safety, and his strong opposition to what he called "shooting a covey to pieces." I don't remember that we were much of a threat, but he didn't like people who did.

Hunting made a stronger impression. Before long I was interested in bigger game than quail, something wilder and deeper in the woods than my father had the time or inclination to pursue. I missed my grandfather then, thinking what a fine thing it would have been to have had a spry old man smelling of pipe tobacco and faintly at times of whiskey who knew how to call a gobbler and to read deer trails in the Pee Dee River Swamp. I realize that I'm describing Robert Ruark's Old Man and not what my own grandfather would have been, but that's because I started reading "The Old Man and the Boy" in *Field and Stream* when I was eleven or twelve. At the end of one of the stories Ruark says, "I've seen a lot of silly damned fools misusing guns and scaring the daylights out of careful people. But they never had the Old Man for a tutor. Some people ain't as lucky as others." There was no doubt in my mind that I was among the unlucky ones, for I had lost the one grandfather who might have been, the hale, vigorous one, the one for whom I was named, lover of horses and hunter. And the other was a frail invalid, impotent in his bed a hundred and fifty miles away.

I

It's hard to give a true account of the way I felt about killing deer during the first two or three years I hunted because my feelings kept changing as light does on a partly cloudy day. I don't want to exaggerate the remorse, but I need to admit that though I never

minded shooting birds, the dying of a buck was another thing, a
resignation, somehow more conclusive. Even so, I could live with
it most of the time, insisting that the process of converting a live
animal into good red table meat was therapeutic for a man who
trades in images and ideas. It was when I failed to make a clean,
quick kill that I suffered. Following a crippled animal through
bare woods, especially when the weather was too warm for December and a damp wind was blowing out of the east, I would lose
command of every logical argument I had devised. Neither the
likelihood of ultimate disease nor the dumb fall of every steer in
Chicago could justify the pain and terror I had caused. When I
was able finally to overtake the deer, I would find myself muttering, "This is a sorry business." When the animal was dead I felt
better. "The bad part is over now," I would say. "All I have to do
now is gut it and drag it out," and I would look forward to the labor
and exhaustion.

That didn't happen often, but two or three occasions were
enough to make me realize that the rationale by which I managed
under ordinary conditions was too brittle to withstand the impact
of an animal's unnecessary suffering. Hunting had brought me
into a deeply satisfying relationship with other men and with the
woods, but I began to believe that if I was going to continue beyond the first excitement I would need a stronger justification.
Billy's example was of little help. For three years I had followed
in his wake, trying to imitate the beautiful intensity of his con-
centration upon the here and now and his uncanny ability to
strike at the right instant with the resolution of a hawk. But I
could not achieve that. As Fenimore Cooper's Natty Bumppo says
of his Indian friend Chingachgook, his gifts were different, be-
stowed by a tradition of hunting that was as deeply ingrained in

his family's way of life as Sunday worship was in mine. When Billy told me he killed his first big game in the company of the men of his mother's family, I began to realize how fully I accepted the authority of tradition. His hunting was an unself-conscious extension into the suburban world of an activity ratified by generations of Claypooles. But as a college professor who taught Sunday school and coached Little League baseball in a town where none of my people had ever lived, I could appeal to nothing that might account for a big, rank buck folded into the back of the family station wagon.

Then, when it mattered most, I caught a glimpse of my grandfather's face. I'm speaking of the other grandfather, the distant invalid. His name was Bob Lawton, but his grandchildren called him Doc. Formerly a Methodist preacher and a professor of Bible and literature, he was confined to his bed for the last thirty years of his life—*invalid*, as though no good for anything, yet a man of uncommon sweetness. As a child, I didn't know what was wrong with him. The only thing I could see was an ingrown big toenail that never healed. Once when I was very young I asked my mother if it was the toe that kept him from walking. She said, "No, Doc's been sick a long time," as though that explained it. It didn't occur to me, of course, that he might ever have been a hunter.

We visited my grandmother and him twice a year—two weeks in the summer and a few days after Christmas. During the long periods between, he occurred in my imagination as a blurred combination of Abraham Lincoln and God, frail and haloed, but each time I returned to his room he greeted me with a cackle of delight that restored to me in an instant the real Doc—the kind face in green light beneath the transparent green visor he wore and the fine splotched hands. It was hard to separate those hands from his voice because they were constantly in action as he talked, shaping phrases, lifting images and turning them in the light of his imagination. I would sit for an hour or more at a time, uncomfortable on the edge of his bed but captivated by the hands and the soft, low-country rhythms of his talking.

As much as he loved baseball he refused to watch a televised game on Sunday afternoon, because his illness, he said, left him so few ways of keeping the Sabbath holy. The rest of us were allowed to take the TV into another room, but I always chose to stay with him. His conversation might cover a range of topics as diverse as the pennant race, the Democratic convention, race relations, fishing, and the Bible. In 1954, when I was thirteen, the *Brown* v. *Board of Education* decision was on his mind. Having heard only the angry reactions of people in my town, I was stunned by his defense of the Supreme Court. "I don't see any way we can justify our treatment of colored people, son." If his sons-in-law were still in the room they might decide they were interested in the baseball game after all. "And the worst of it may be that we have deprived ourselves of the things they might have taught us." I suppose I had never considered the possibility of learning anything from black people except maybe how to catch a 'coon, but I would listen as he told me about Ike, a black boy with whom he had grown up on a plantation in Hampton County. Almost exactly the same age, they had been inseparable as boys, fishing a black-water stream in a cypress bottom called Boggy Gut. Once, when he was twelve, Doc "stumped" his toe, as he put it, and swore prodigiously. Ike called his attention to what he was saying so that he was able to hear himself through the ears of another person, and he was so ashamed that he vowed never to use profanity again.

The Civil War was as real to him as the empty sleeves and trouser legs of the old men in his family. It was too bad, he would say, that the South had not produced a Tolstoy, especially since we had had the soldiers and the war. He thought it must be easier to make a great war than a great book.

Then I might hear a little lecture on Shakespearean tragedy or *Paradise Lost* or the odes of John Keats. Interested as much in the poet as in his work, he would tell me of Keats's last, sad days in Rome and say that he was a brave young man, "little more than a boy, and deeply in love with a girl he knew he could never see again." For no apparent reason, he would wonder if Ike was doing well. They had kept in touch as long as Doc had been able to visit his family in Hampton County, but he hadn't been home in years. Boggy *had* been a fine place to fish, he'd say. Sometimes when they used to visit his family, he would get out of the car at the bridge as they drove in, send his wife and children on to his mother's house, and spend an hour on the stream, using a sapling for a pole and "stringing" his fish on a forked stick. When he came walking up to the house in muddy shoes, clutching his stick of redbreasts, the servants would laugh, "Mr. Robbie *sho* do love his fishing." I now have a photograph of him fishing on Boggy in a coat and tie, but as a child my imagination wasn't up to the task of featuring Doc as a young man.

He would ask me if I liked to fish.

"Yes sir."

"It's a fine thing, lad. You know our Lord approved of fishermen. You remember when the disciples saw him walking on the shore of the Sea of Galilee after the Resurrection and he told them to cast their nets on the other side?" Then he would wave his dry stick of an arm as though to push aside a curtain and reveal to me the Jesus he could see, walking like a barefoot boy on the wet

beach in the first light of morning. I would lose touch with everything but the hands and the voice, lose the features of his face in
the green shade of the visor, and even doubt that there was anything under the covers. Then, shifting my weight to get a better
purchase on the edge of the bed, I would pull the blanket tight
against the ingrown nail of that appalling toe, and he would cry
out, not loud but hurt, and remind me gently of the ills the flesh
is heir to.

Besides telling me about Ike and Boggy Gut, Doc did not
speak of his childhood; I don't think I ever heard him mention his
father. What I knew of his early life I learned mostly from my
mother. As a girl she had spent summer vacations with the relatives in Hampton County. At times she would entertain my
brother and sisters and me by telling of how she had played with
her cousins, hiding in upstairs rooms of the big house, racing
barefoot down the white sandy road that led to the servants' quarters, or climbing among the massive limbs of the live oaks in the
yard. Out of such details my imagination fashioned a scene like
the one depicted on the label of Deep South jelly—a columned
mansion half-hidden by semitropical growth; the sun shown upon
it, and through the open kitchen window you could hear a painted
bunting singing in the garden.

Long since enamored of the low country, I couldn't understand
why Doc had left it to spend his life among the eroded, red-clay
hills of the upper part of the state. "Because he was called to
preach, I suppose," my mother said. Indifferent to the prestige of
a big pulpit, she continued, he told the Lord he could be happy
in a mud puddle. "As long as there weren't mosquitoes in it," my
father added. He thought Doc had left home because of the ma-
laria that had plagued his childhood. "Doc's scared to death of a

mosquito," he said. But my mother observed that while her mother, like a cat, loved a place, Doc had always liked to move. They had lived in seven different houses during her childhood. "He never got attached to anywhere," she said.

I was teaching William Faulkner's story "The Bear" to a class of unresponsive sophomores one day; trying to recall my own re-action to the story at their age, I suddenly remembered that I had once read it aloud to my grandfather. He had asked what I was studying in my English classes, and I had mentioned Faulkner. He had been hearing a great deal about this Faulkner, he said; what did I think of him? So I opened the book. "There was a man and a dog too this time," I began. He wouldn't let me stop until I finished the third chapter. When I read the passage about hounds baying game through the riverswamp, he cackled with delight, nodding his head in recognition, approving Faulkner's descrip-tion of something I had thought he knew nothing of.

After that recollection I went to see my grandmother as soon as I could. She was much frailer than she had been in the days of my visits from college but still a pert wren of a lady whose eyes danced when I asked about Doc. "Oh, Bob loved to hunt," she said as though surprised I needed to ask. After a pause she laughed. "He took me hunting with him only one time. I don't think he ever wanted to take me after that. We had gone down to Garnett for Christmas. That was the first Christmas after we were married." Another pause. "We were married on my birthday, you know."

"Yes ma'am."

"We wanted to get married that summer when I was seventeen, but my father and mother wouldn't hear of it. They said seventeen was too young so we had to wait until September 15 when I was eighteen. In that little church at Glenn Springs. You remember that little white church?"

I had never been to Glenn Springs, but I said, "Yes ma'am. And it was the Christmas after that?" For a moment she seemed confused, but then her face cleared. "Seems like they were always having deer drives and dove shoots down there, going bird hunting, that sort of thing. Well I wanted to go on the deer drive." She chuckled to herself. "I had no more business going on that deer drive than flying to the moon, but nothing would do but for me to go. I think Bob must have been embarrassed 'cause ladies didn't do that sort of thing in those days, but he gave in and dressed me up in some of his old clothes. I must have looked a sight. We met for breakfast while it was still dark, over at Brewton's house. You know Uncle Brew's house? And we could hear the people hitching up the wagons outside while we were eating, and the dogs barking and the horses.

"Bob and I rode to the swamp in a wagon, but most of the men went on horseback. It was so dark and cold I was afraid to get out, but 'course Bob knew exactly where we were going. We no sooner got in the woods when we heard the dogs. You know how they do, don't you? They'd sound like they were coming straight toward us. Then it would sound like they'd swung away and after a while you could hardly hear them at all. Then in a little bit they'd start getting closer again. Bob kept telling me what the buck was doing, and it was like I could see him, tearing along out in front of those hounds.

"Before long they started getting so close I thought I would perish from excitement. The woods just seemed to be full of dogs, and then I could see the tops of the cane swishing back and forth where they were coming through the thicket. But when that little deer came bounding out, I felt so sorry for it. I said, 'Bob, you know you're not going to shoot that little deer.'" My grandmother laughed as though at her own silliness.

"What did Doc do?" I asked.

"He didn't pay me any more attention than if I had been a stump. I could tell by the expression on his face that he wasn't hearing a word I was saying.

"I wept so over that little deer. I was trying to shoo the dogs back and Bob kept blowing his horn for the other men to come up. I don't think he thought I was going to make much of a hunter after that."

"Was it a small deer?" I asked.

She laughed. "Well, it looked small to me."

"What about the rack, the antlers?"

"Oh, I don't remember, son. It had antlers. I know that."

"How long did Doc hunt after y'all were married?"

"He hunted up until the time he was too sick to go anymore. Even after he had to go to bed, he'd get me to take him out to a field near our house so he could shoot doves. I'd set his chair up in a blind on the edge of the field, and then I'd pick up his birds for him." ·

"Was he a good shot?"

"I don't think he ever missed. I'm sure he must have, but it didn't look like it to me. We used to have some good dove suppers. Do you like doves?"

But I was back in the swamp, intent upon the face she saw when she asked him not to shoot the deer. It was a thin, scholarly face in gold-rimmed glasses, but there was a resolution in it that set me free.

II

In a tree stand at Groton. September 1975.

The red sun drops below the tree line of the Savannah River bottoms. The air is heavy and still but a little cooler now. I hear no sound that is not natural, no tires singing on a distant highway, no boats on the river, no chain saws, tractors, airplanes, or banging doors but only the tedious sawing of insects, literally millions thick in the tall grass around my stand, and the occasional querulous chirp of a towhee looking for a place to go to bed. You notice the bird, but the monotone of the insects is so constant that you have to remind yourself to listen, just as you have to make a conscious effort to look at the blue air. As far as I can see in all directions the landscape is broken with woods and fields: in front of me the deep blue wall of the riverswamp, to the right patches of abandoned fields, open pines, and dense pine plantations; a dark stand of mature loblolly just over my shoulder; and off to the left, stretching away to the haze of distant trees, a long field of soybeans, yellow and chewed at the edges by deer.

Those trees are standing just across the line in Hampton County. Though I do not know where my grandfather lived, I suspect he may have known this place. My grandmother said they hunted in the swamp. She must have meant this riverbottom forest, maybe a few miles south of here. It would be nice to think that he hunted here on Groton where I am now a paying guest of northern landlords.

It's not that I resent the owners. They have been paying taxes on this land for seventy-five years, and they have been better stewards as far as my interests are concerned than many of the local farmers. But I feel I am *of* this country in a way that they cannot be, that even though Darlington is across the state from Groton this is still my brier patch, so to speak, and I'd like to have some certain knowledge of that.

This is the right time for deer. They should be slipping from the swamp now, coming to the soybeans on the hill. The does and young bucks move first. The old bucks will wait until dark. I survey the edge of the swamp with my glasses. They wait much later, I won't be able to see to shoot. Unless a buck walks under my stand. I look down. *Three does*, right there, poised, nervous. I am amazed. *Where do they come from*, I wonder, *how do they slip up so quietly?* Then I see the tombstones. The deer are standing in a little graveyard almost directly beneath my stand. I count six stones, four in a row and two behind, plain slabs stained the color of earth and half-hidden by the dying grass. I unload my rifle, jacking the bullets from the magazine carefully so that they won't fall and be lost in the grass below. But I lose two despite the effort, for I am eager to get down while the light is still strong enough to read by. At the first sound of the rifle's action the deer bolt, flags bounding high above the grass, brilliant in the dusk.

I kneel before a tombstone, a little conscious of snakes. *Sacred to the memory of DAVID DELOACH who departed this life July 13 1815, aged 63 yrs*. Beside him *REBECKAH, wife of David Deloach, who departed this life Oct. 10 1807, aged 40 years*. Where and how did these people live? I wondered. Somewhere nearby, perhaps in sight of this place. The other two stones mark the graves of James Deloach who died in 1824 at the age of twenty-seven (obviously a son of David and Rebeckah) and his wife Sarah who died the following year. The stones on the second row are those of infants, David (Feb. 1795) and Jephthah (Mar. 1805), apparently sons also of David and Rebeckah. And then I notice a

marker I didn't see from the stand, off to the side. I go over to it.
It's almost too dark to read now. My fingertips trace the cool
braille on its face:

Sacred
to the memory of
ELEVIA DELOACH
wife of
Wm. B. Deloach
who departed this life
Nov. 27th 1822
in the 18th year of her age.

The air thickens. Shadows gather. I can't make out their faces, but
I see them huddled in a slow November rain, and I hear the
bride's ethereal name uttered upon this air. And it occurs to me
that every acre of this plantation is rustling with ghostly gestures
of labor and marriage and childbearing and maybe war and all
kinds of dying.

Approaching headlights glow beneath a distant fall of land.
Presently I hear the rattle of the pickup and move on out to the
road. I'm going to find out who these people were.

I wondered from the beginning if they were connected with my
family. The Lawtons were a prolific clan, scattered for miles along
the lower Savannah River. But I found no familiar names in any of
the old graveyards on Groton. I was only a little disappointed, for
I was not interested so much in doing a *Roots* project as I was in
learning about the history of the country I was hunting. It would
be nice, I thought, to know that this place was once owned by

people connected with mine. For some reason. But it seemed unlikely.

Then I met a man who had done extensive research on our family: a distant Lawton cousin, practicing law in a nearby town.

"Long as you're stomping around out there," he said, "see if you can find James Thomson's grave."

"Who is James Thomson?" I asked.

"Early settler. Revolutionary colonel. An ancestor of ours, you know. He was a big somebody around here."

Having written a monograph on Thomson, this cousin had learned all there was to know about him, but he couldn't remember the location of his grave. He had been to it only once, and that as a child. He recalled no tombstones. Except for the memory of one person, as things turned out, that unmarked burial site may have been lost forever, but the person who remembered was old George Frazier. Because of his age he was the one I asked. "Yes suh. I know 'zackly where dat grabeya'd at."

He led me to it on a hot, steamy day in July, angling toward the dark wall of the swamp through an old field grown up in broomsedge and pine.

"Watch your foots, suh," George warned. "Old rattler bad een here."

I stumbled to keep up, snarling my ankles in briers again and again.

This had been wilderness when James Thomson came into it in 1765, a vast open grove of great pines and here and there amid them the mysterious circular ponds called Carolina bays. He had come in his middle years like a vigorous Abraham with family and herds, bondservants and household gods, and stopped at the edge

of the swamp. No sooner had he cleared the land and planted it
when the Revolution broke out. The fighting in this part of the
country was not a clash of armies but bloody civil strife, Tory and
Patriot neighbors attacking and burning each other's cabins,
slaughtering livestock and sometimes women and children. James
Thomson commanded a company of light-horse militia, guarding
the river crossings against Tory raiders from Georgia. By the end
of the war he was promoted to the rank of colonel. His one surviv-
ing letter reveals a man of considerable education for that time
and place. To General Benjamin Lincoln he wrote:

> I was yesterday within a few miles of Pocataligo, but could
> hear no certainty where either of the Armies are. Was informed
> by a Prisoner Escaped from the British Army that there was at
> that Place about 300 Light Horse. British. and some foot. My
> orders is to raise as many horse as possible & Endeavor to pre-
> vent their Plundering parties from Ravaging the Country. mine
> is Lowest Guard on this side the River. not knowing when I
> may receive any Orders from my field officers I'd be glad to Re-
> ceive any Instruction from you that you think Necessary in the
> Present Situation.

George Frazier was standing at the edge of the swamp in the
shade of moss-draped oaks. In just such a place, I thought, on a
bright Sunday morning in May, James Thomson finished that letter and signed it with a modest flourish. I easily featured a
stretched tarp and seated beneath it in a pieced-together uniform
the man, thick and capable, his thin brown hair pulled back in a
tight pigtail and no nonsense at all in his face.

"Dere it," George said and pointed out an almost imperceptible elevation, fifteen square feet in area, and bordered on all sides by the vestige of a shallow trench. I asked him how he had learned of it.

"Man name Hershel. Plowing chufas back here one day. Seen a toonstone standing over here in dese trees. Said 'What een de hell white folks burying way back here for?'"

"There was a tombstone here?"

"Right here, suh, where Hershel saw it."

"How long ago was that?" I asked.

"Long time, suh, I don't know. Long time back."

George Frazier's face was as small and tight as a fist. I had no idea what he was thinking. Probably wondering what in the hell this white man was doing in the wilting heat of July, looking for a grave way back here. I might have told him that that was my granddaddy buried there, and that I was about to inherit the plantation from him, but not to worry he would be free to stay on. Because that's what I was thinking.

For a long time I, who owned only an acre of rocky clay in an Athens subdivision, had thought that hunting was a good way of gaining the intimate knowledge of a locale that amounts to a kind of ownership. I had taken a smug pleasure at times in realizing that I knew some of the farms where I hunted better than the people who held title to them. Thus loved them more. But that way of knowing and loving and having would not be enough for me here at Groton, for other men hunted on the plantation, and some knew its woods and fields more intimately than I did. What I sought was a knowledge that would give me an exclusive claim to it. In the fact of my own blood here, I believed I had found what I was looking for, a world intact and deep in time that was mine to enter as I pleased.

But instead of assuring George Frazier that he would be allowed to stay on, I just told him that this James Thomson was the original settler, a Revolutionary soldier, and a member of the state legislature. "This was all cleared in those days, George. There was a cabin here and servants' quarters and barns and pens and cotton and corn patches, and over yonder where Three Bridge Branch comes into the swamp he had a grist mill. He was a big somebody around here back then."

George Frazier looked at me with that closed black fist of a face. "Sho hard to tell it now, ain't it, suh?"

As I shared my discovery with members of the club, I began to see that the experience of the plantation I had sought was exclusive in a way I had not expected. Encountering one bored expression after another, I was puzzled to the point of consternation. By coincidence I had been propelled into the echoing chambers of my own ancestry, and they seemed unable to appreciate the significance of that.

"Look," I said to Charlie Creedmore one day, "you come into a place like this when you're thirty-five years old as a member of a hunting club. You get to know it and you learn to love it and you even wish you could have it because it's so close to what you've always dreamed of, and *then* you find out that the people who do own it, own it because your family sold it to them. That it was your own family that first settled the place and named it and fought for it and planted it and hunted it, so that a big part of who you are must have been bred right here. Out of all the people I've ever known in my life, I don't know a single one of them who has had anything like that happen to him."

Charlie said, no, he didn't reckon he did either.

So I decided it would take a book to explain what I was doing, a history of the small plantations Groton once had been—collectively a garden, wrought out of wilderness by people who happened to have been my progenitors, held by them awhile, and somehow finally lost. With that purpose in mind I began to work in the Hampton County courthouse and at the Caroliniana Library in Columbia; I visited distant relatives and wrote to others; and at Groton I spent more time gathering information than hunting in the swamp. For I was trying in some sense really to recover something, and the book was to be the means by which I certified my title. It came to matter more than any buck.

One of the kinsmen I met was a first cousin of my mother's, an old widower living a few miles below Groton in an unpainted, two-story house built by his father in 1905. His name was King Maner. One year after George Frazier led me through the briers to James Thomson's grave, I went with King to another family landmark. It stood in a grove of live oaks a few miles south of Groton at the village of Robertville. Though the day was hot, King wore a coat and tie. No matter that the coat was baggy and the tie stained, the code he lived by required that a gentleman be so dressed when he left his house. And King was a gentleman. I followed him from the car into the shade beneath the trees. He stopped before a set of pillared steps and rested his hand upon what was left of a newel post. The steps were ornate, fashioned of brick and sculptured mortar, and they ascended to empty air. King spoke in the heavy low-country brogue you hear only from people who learned to talk before the advent of radio. "Now they tell me, Jim, that this was the house of our great, great grandfather."

"Is that right? I thought it was John G. Lawton's house."

"I don't know now. That's just what I've heard, that it was built by William Henry Lawton."

"I read somewhere that it had twenty-one rooms."

"Twenty-one rooms," King said. "Imagine that."

"Have you ever heard what the name of this plantation was?"

"No, son, I haven't. You know more about these old places than I do, and I've lived here all my life."

A rank growth of privet had loosened the bricks of the steps. I climbed them anyway until I was high enough to look out from the shade of the live oaks upon the white glare of a soybean field.

Sherman.

Riding north out of Robertville in January of 1865, his cavalry under the command of mad Kilpatrick, he burned almost every big house on the Augusta Road as far as the upper end of Groton—burned Benjamin Bostick's Ingleside with its famous formal gardens, Francis Maner's Gayfield, William J. Lawton's Gravel Hill, and Doc's grandfather's plantation, Cypress Vale. An itinerant Methodist preacher wrote in his book *Stray Leaves* that after the war he found Joseph Maner Lawton's widow "living in what had been a servant's house, near where her noble mansion once stood." That woman, Elizabeth Thomson Lawton, was the granddaughter of Colonel James Thomson. Her youngest son— Doc's father—was living with her, eighteen-year-old Maner Lawton, wondering how he was going to spend the rest of his life now that the Yankees had come.

The soybean field stretched before me, as boring as a linoleum floor, but beneath its white glare lay a ruined garden, grown up in beggar lice and broomsedge, legacy of the war to Maner Lawton and his Bostick and Maner cousins. He did as well as he could with it, I guessed, but he never called it Cypress Vale. By the end of the century he was one of the few members of the clan who had not sold their farms to northern sportsmen like the Belmonts and the Winthrops.

I came down from the steps and joined the old man.

"They tell me my father owned some of that Winthrop place at one time, Jim." I recalled the deed I had read in the Hampton County courthouse: James K. Maner to Robert Dudley Winthrop, two thousand acres, bounded on the north by Peeples, on the east and south by Winthrop, and on the west by the Savannah River—Old Greenwood Plantation, settled before the Revolution by David Deloach, named by William who buried his wife and children there, burned by Sherman, and purchased sometime after the war by James K. and his brother W. F. Maner, *to* Robert Dudley Winthrop in consideration of the sum of sixteen thousand dollars.

"Eight dollars an acre," King said. "Think of that. What year was that, Jim?"

"Probably 1907, '08," I said.

"Well, that's about right. My father died in 1911. The money from that land is probably what my mother lived on all those years. Sixteen thousand dollars would go a long way in those days."

As we were walking toward the car, I remembered my grandmother's story. "You reckon they ever hunted deer up there? I mean your father and Doc and Uncle Brewton and them?"

"I wouldn't think so, son. My father and my uncle Frank were turpentining up there and sawmilling too, I think. I know they did a good deal of hunting, but I wouldn't think they did it up there."

III

In the swamp at Groton. November 1977.

It was raining hard when I went to bed last night. I woke up once during the early morning and listened to its drumming on the roof. I thought then that we wouldn't hunt today, but it had stopped when we got up. I find the tree I'm looking for. Its roots are flaring buttresses that enclose me on either side when I settle in. It should be getting light on the hill, even with this cloud cover, but it's still too early to see in the swamp. I can hardly distinguish tree trunks forty yards away. The woods are perfectly still except for the dripping. The wet leaves beneath me soak through the seat of my pants. I won't sit here long past daylight. The radio said a front is coming through today, clearing in the afternoon and turning real cold tonight. Tomorrow morning ought to be perfect if it's not too windy.

A buck crosses the corner of a field of soybeans in the wet gray dawn. The stalks are dead and dark with rain. He walks deliberately, with his head down, against the rows. At the edge of open pinewoods he stops and looks over his shoulder, back toward the southeast, as though he were trying to smell the coming light. The wind is drifting out of the east.

I'd almost as soon not kill a deer this morning, and I'm not sure why. I guess the big buck I shot last month pretty much finished the season for me.

The buck stands in the wet grass on a little hill above a sandy road. He would rather quarter into the wind, but he wants does and he wants acorns, and the two converge in one desire as he looks toward the swamp. He hears the rattle and bounce of a vehicle and turns his head in that direction, ears pricked forward. As the headlights sweep his body, he launches into flight, clearing the road easily in full stride before the oncoming truck, and plunges into a dense stand of young pines. The driver hits his brakes. "Godamighty did you see that!" His partner says he saw a deer but he couldn't tell what it was. "Damn thing had a rack on him like this," the driver says and spreads his hands as far as the cab will allow. His partner doesn't see how you can tell in this light.

This was the swamp section of old Greenwood. King Maner's father, Cousin Jimmy, must have logged these very woods around the turn of the century. In spite of what King says, I'm going to fancy that Doc hunted right here, at least once.

It is still dark in the pine thicket. The buck relaxes, nosing the pinestraw for mushrooms and doe scent. He moves slowly, ambling first in one direction then in another but always generally toward the swamp. Sometimes he stops and stands still, his head up, listening. The thicket grows dim with filtered light.

A wide circle of bare trees leans in upon me, dissolved in the dripping dawn. The open grove is hedged on one side by a thicket of cane, a pale green swath a hundred and fifty yards in front of me. I take out a handkerchief and wipe the moisture from the lens of my scope and from the barrel of my rifle. I can think of a dozen questions I would like to ask my grandfather. I can be sure at least that he visited this place when he was a boy because his uncle's family lived right here at what was once Oakland Plantation. Then a voice, quiet and even upon the damp air: "Why does it matter?" I look up. A man is sitting in front of me. He is about my age and thin, and he is wearing gold-rimmed glasses.

"Doc?"

"What difference does it make, son?"

"I'm not really sure. Sir. I used to read stories when I was a child about a boy who hunted and fished with his grandfather. Then I found out how close we came. I mean, all we needed was for you to have been well. I guess I felt cheated. And now here I am, right here where it all started for you. I reckon I'm trying to force things together. But the hunting—the sense I have of our almost hunting together—is just a way of grabbing hold of something bigger, of this whole world down here. I don't know. Maybe if I could believe that we sort of hunted together here, I could recover what you . . . "

"Turned my back on?"

"Well, I don't think I would put it that way, but there seems to have been a detachment from it that I don't understand. I have a friend named Rick who grew up hunting with his grandfather on an old family plantation over near Sumter—exactly the kind of thing I always wanted, longed for. A couple of years ago his family lost the place, but instead of being devastated by that, as you would expect, he seemed resigned to it. In fact, he told me that he was upset mainly for the sake of an old black couple who had lived there all their lives and were going to have to move. That happened at the same time I started hunting down here. It seemed to me that Rick was almost casual about losing the very thing I was suddenly desperate to get my hands on."

The buck steps from the pine thicket and crosses the harrowed ground of a firebreak into a chest-high stand of cane that fringes the bank above the swamp. Before him lies an expanse of flooded timber, dark and luminous in the early light. He lowers his heavy, royal head and scratches at a place behind his ear with a hind foot. Then he starts down the slick embankment, his splayed hooves scoring the clay as he slides into the water. It is belly-deep against the hill, but he goes bounding through it quietly toward the higher ground within the swamp.

"The old black woman was even more casual about it. Rick used to ask me down to shoot ducks a couple of times a season, and I had an opportunity to get to know her a little. Her name was Alice. On what turned out to be our last hunt down there, I was supposed to meet Rick at Alice's house, but I got there before he did. So I left my car in the yard and walked on down to the branch to see if I could kill a duck or two before dark.

"You can imagine the kind of place it was—a little better than most sharecroppers' cabins but unpainted, with an old fyce dog up under the porch and a yard full of chickens and a grove of chinaberry trees close enough to the back door to catch the dishwater every day. Alice was sitting in the doorway of an outbuilding when I pulled up—a tiny woman all bundled up against the late afternoon cold—it was a raw day, like this—wearing an old coat and hat that looked like the kind of thing her husband had used to wear to church, and shelling corn into a white porcelain pan. Her husband wasn't there. I told her who I was and to tell Rick I'd be back around dark.

"I killed a couple of ducks that evening but got wet up to my waist retrieving them and had a cold walk back. You know what it's like walking across a wet field in the dark toward the yellow glow of someone's window a long way off. The dog started barking at me before I got to the yard. Rick still wasn't there, and I was cold and wanted a cup of coffee so I put the ducks on top of my car and got some instant out of a sack of groceries I had brought and went up and rapped on the door.

"Alice was glad for me to use her stove to heat water and she gave me a cup for the coffee. Then she invited me up to the front room to drink it. That was the only room in the house that was heated, and it hit me like a furnace when I walked in. Not just the heat but the colors too, a confusion of pink and orange, crowded with tables and beds and chests of drawers. For all that furniture it was hard to find a place to sit so I stood for as long as I could stand it in front of the gas heater, drying out. The walls were covered with family photographs—you've seen them—young glossy black faces in army uniforms—that sort of thing. And there was a funeral-home calendar with a technicolor picture of 'Behold I stand at the door and knock' and, the only thing that really surprised me in that house, a framed *Life* magazine cover of Martin Luther King.

"A card table in the middle of the room was covered with books—a Bible or two, some kind of lesson material and what looked like a concordance. Alice explained that she was preparing her Sunday school lesson. It was on the raising of Lazarus. No, she wasn't the teacher. Wasn't qualified to teach, she said, just doing her lesson. Her Bible was an old King James. I asked her what she thought of some of the recent translations. She said she reckoned they were all right, and then she picked up the King James and said, 'But this how my Jesus talk to me.'

"Rick didn't get in until late that night so Alice and I had a long visit. She talked mostly about the changes she had seen in recent years—no more cotton, her children going up the road, the church drying up—'all old peoples now,' she said. And she talked freely about the civil rights movement. Martin Luther King had made things a lot better for 'the colored,' she said, 'but Jesus free us all when he raise from the dead.' I couldn't tell whether she was talking about Lazarus or the Resurrection, but I didn't ask for clarification.

"I could see why Rick was upset about their having to move. Alice told me she had been born in a cabin that sat on that very spot. The present house had been built after the cabin burned, and she and David had brought up all their children there. Buried two of them in the churchyard down the road. I don't think I've ever seen anyone who belonged more thoroughly to a place. You'd think it would kill her to have to leave, but she said she was 'just a sojourner passin' through'; it might be hard to get used to the traffic and noise in town after having lived in the country all her life, but town 'just another little stoppin' off place,' and Jesus was going to see them through."

"And that's what you don't understand?"

"I just mean that I can't achieve that kind of detachment myself. Seems to me that home amounts to a whole lot more when it happens in a place like that, or like down here, especially the way it was seventy-five years ago, with cousins in every house and a graveyard full of family. It's hard for me to see anything wrong with loving such a place and even fighting to hold on to it, the way James Thomson did and your uncles and cousins in 1861."

The buck comes out of the water onto dry ground and catches a whiff of does in heat and lifts his flared nostrils to the damp breeze. Up ahead he sees the naked wood of a familiar sapling. The hair on his back stands up and he trots toward it. The sapling is scraped clean of bark as high as a man's waist. The buck lowers his rack before it, cradles it in a junction of tine and beam and moves his weight against it, scraping upward as he leans into it, and the gnurled antler abrades the wood.

"Maybe you've heard that I did a lot of deer hunting. I loved it when I was a boy. But, you know, Annie made me stop and think about that thing. She never tried to stop me, but I could see that it troubled her. What I finally came to understand is, that it was all right for me to shoot a buck as long as I knew I didn't have to do it."

"But how can you know that?"

"Sometimes, I imagine, the only way you can find out is by not doing it."

The buck has a scrape beneath the branch of a chestnut oak on the other side of the thicket. He lowers his head and grunts and enters the cane.

"And what if you go ahead and take the buck anyway?"

"That is arrogance. And arrogance can neither know nor love, hence not inherit and so have nothing to bequeath."

"So you would say it *is* the meek who inherit the earth?"

"If you will consider your friend Alice I think you'll see that it is only the meek who can."

I am about to ask if it is possible to inherit the earth by writing a book, but at that moment I see the buck. It steps from the wall of cane and stands with its head up. I reach for my binoculars and discover that I have left them, so I raise my rifle to use the scope. The buck doesn't seem unusually big, but I have never seen such an extravagant crown. Even at this distance I can tell that it is wide and heavy. I am trembling a little, but I know already that I'll not shoot him. If a mounted head makes a statement, it is not one that needs to be repeated.

So I stand up, carefully but not caring, and lean against the tree. The buck does not see me. He starts forward, walking through the grove. I hold the cross hairs on him. Forty yards away he stops, looks at me and stamps his hoof. I could kill him easily.

He starts forward again, wholly intent on the strange, offensive shape I represent. With every step or two he stops, confused, throws up his head and moves it from side to side. My arms ache from the weight of the rifle, but I want to see how close he will come and cannot risk any movement.

Suddenly the buck turns and circles to my right, seeking confirmation through his nose that I am alien and dangerous. In profile his tines seem even higher than I had thought. Slowly I lower my rifle to comprehend the entire animal. The dark body is smaller than you would expect. His step is quick and light, and he tosses his head as though annoyed by insects, but he is really trying to wind me.

He passes behind a big oak. When he appears on the other side he stops and faces me, ten steps away. His nostrils are flaring and I can see shredded bark clogging the gnurled base of the antlers. I think I will kill him after all. He is all aquiver, already gathering himself. Slowly I bring my rifle to my shoulder. And the buck lifts himself with great power, twisting his body in the air like a diver, and thunders away with a flinging of dirt, down through the dim, narrow reaches of the swamp.

I find a place to sit and light a cigarette, choosing not to think of anything at all.

9
Isaac's Blessing

ANYONE WHO HUNTS IS FAMILIAR with the smell of old hunting clothes. It varies a little in accordance with the man who wears them and the country he hunts, but it is always an outdoor smell—in my own clothes, something like a taste of wind blowing through dead corn, faintly mixed with a musky animal odor. Sometimes in summer, coming upon a well-used hunting jacket hanging in the basement, I have held its rough fabric to my face and inhaled the richness of a wet winter field.

It must have been such a smell that pleased blind Isaac when he embraced his son. Kissing him on the cheek and neck, he said, "Ah, the smell of my son is like the smell of a field the Lord has blessed."

That son was the wrong one, of course. Isaac had summoned Esau the hunter to receive his blessing as firstborn. Before bestowing it, he asked Esau to go into the field with his bow and hunt some wild game so that he might prepare for his father the savory stew that he loved. Isaac's wife, Rebeckah, overhearing these arrangements, directed Jacob, whom she favored, to dress in Esau's hunting clothes and to cover his arms and neck with the hairy skins of kids. Then, handing him a bowl of goat stew, she pushed him trembling into his father's tent. The stew must have sloshed onto the floor as Jacob announced his presence. Isaac was surprised that Esau could have returned so quickly, and he was skeptical of the voice, but the hairy hands and, especially, the smell of the robe convinced him.

The fact that it was the wrong son does not impair the beauty of his words: "May the Lord give you of heaven's dew and of earth's richness—an abundance of grain and new wine." Isaac meant to bless Esau rather than Jacob—not because Esau was a hunter but because he was firstborn. My firstborn is the only son I have, and like Esau he is a hunter. That's reason enough for me to love what Isaac says, even if he is deceived into saying it to the imposter.

John took to hunting at an early age, as eagerly as a lab pup, naturally loving the chase and the country it took him into. I was concerned at first that he might not be able to manage the killing, for he had a gentle spirit and a strong affection for animals. But when the time came he accepted that part of it too. At least, he seemed to. But fathers often don't see clearly when they are looking at their children. And maybe that also is one of the things the story of Isaac's blessing is about.

I took John to Groton for the first time when he was twelve. As we turned off the highway onto the sandy road that led to the cabin, I told him that the plantation was his ancestral ground, for a hundred and fifty years the estate of Thomsons and Lawtons and Maners, and that he was the eighth generation of our blood to hunt deer in that place. He seemed to be listening, but when he spoke he asked if I thought it would be easier to kill a buck in the swamp or on the hill. I started to chide him but forced myself to remember that he had been looking forward to this trip for four years with the bright-eyed anticipation of a small child awaiting Christmas. He was coming into the country at last, and though history might someday stir his imagination, right now he was interested only in deer and hogs.

From that time until he finished high school, the annual father-son hunt at Groton was the best weekend of the year for him. Though he never showed much interest in the history of the plantation, he killed a cowhorn spike when he was fourteen with me beside him in a tree stand. That was fine for a while—it was his first antlered buck—but by the following year he was ready for something bigger. I tried to explain to him that the quality of the hunt matters more than the size of the rack. He nodded, but fifteen-year-olds have trouble really believing that, especially if they have not taken a branch-antlered buck. From their point of view, the size of the rack somehow signifies not only the sexual maturity of the buck but, by some mysterious correspondence, the prowess of the hunter as well. He was not the kind to say much about his feelings, but I suspected he was thinking that a big buck would prove to the men in the club that he had become a true hunter. And—I must confess—I was thinking the same way, anxious for my sake as well as his that he take a trophy head.

On Saturday of that weekend we were still waiting, but Billy Claypoole, who had no son of his own, accepted John as a hunter anyway. He did it by proposing, as one man to another, that they go hunting together that afternoon. I was a little surprised when John told me. It is not always a simple matter to take a boy hunting, even one with John's experience, for it requires that you adjust your pace to the boy's, which means that most of the time you don't get to do much hunting yourself. As it turned out, that's not what Billy had in mind anyway; what he proposed was for John to hunt alone. Billy would drop him at the bridge over Clearwater Stream and pick him up at dark. I didn't know what I thought of that. John had never hunted deer by himself, except from a tree stand. While there would be no danger from other hunters in the swamp, because of the established boundaries, the swamp itself was formidable. I wasn't sure that he was ready to take it on.

He and Billy stood in front of me, the boy no more than shoulder-high to the man, brushing his heavy blond hair from his forehead. If he was apprehensive he showed no sign of it. In fact, there seemed to be a conspiratorial smugness between the two, a mutual understanding that since I had always acknowledged Billy's authority in outdoor matters I could hardly oppose him now, and a shared pleasure in knowing that I was aware of my untenable position. I couldn't even tell John to be careful—that would clearly have been a denial of the status Billy had conferred upon him. And they were enjoying *that* too. Even asking him if he had a compass would be a mistake, I knew, not because it suggested a lack of woodcraft—no one went into the swamp without a compass—but because it implied that he was careless enough to have overlooked it, or worse, callow enough to believe he could manage without one. But I heard myself asking. Of course he had a compass, he said.

"Well, wait a minute," I said, "you better take the two-seventy." I fetched the rifle from the gun rack in my truck. "You'll have a better chance of killing him with this."

He said thanks and handed me the thirty-thirty and without looking back followed Billy toward his Blazer. "You know how to load it?" I called.

Without turning, "Yessir."

"And unload it? You have to push that little button in the trigger guard."

He was wearing my Bean boots and my camouflage one-piece. I noticed that it hung loose on his shoulders and bagged a little in the seat. I shivered involuntarily, as though someone had placed a cold hand on the back of my neck.

They did not come in at dark. I stood outside the cabin as winter twilight gathered, reacting to the sound of each vehicle as it came up from the south. Each time it was someone else. By full dark everyone had come in except them. From where I stood outside, I could see people sitting by the fire in the main room of the cabin.

There's no reason to stand around in the cold, I told myself.

But let's see if they had any luck, I argued back. Maybe John killed something—if not a deer maybe a pig.

I sat down on a bench.

Earlier, just before dark, I had heard a shot from the swamp. Since everyone else had been hunting from stands on the hill, I figured it had to be John or Billy who fired, especially now that they were running so late. I tried to picture John with deer in front of him—white tails switching in the cane, a flash of pelage, flank or neck, and the boy trying to decide what and when to shoot. Plantation policy discouraged the killing of a buck with an antler spread of less than sixteen inches. But any branched rack might look like a trophy to him. And if he decided to take a doe, there was always the danger of shooting a button buck instead— even I had made that mistake. If John came in with an unacceptable deer, I could not expect the men in the camp to indulge him because of his age; they would figure if he was old enough to hunt on his own, he was old enough to live with the consequences of his decisions. The thought of it made me shudder.

I stood up and walked around the yard, stamping my feet.

If that late shot had been his, John would have had to return to the bridge and wait for Billy and then, if they made connections, take Billy back to the fallen animal. I knew from my own experience that was hard to do, even in daylight, unless one marked his trail with flagging. And I realized John had taken no flagging. He did carry toilet paper in his possibles bag, but whether or not he would think to use it, I didn't know.

In all that speculation, I realized, I had been assuming he had made a clean kill. It was more likely that he had not, for even when fatally hit, deer often run surprising distances. If that had happened, John would probably have taken off after it. In his excitement he might not have remembered to put the rifle back on safety. I didn't know whether he had a flashlight or not, or a dragging rope. If they were not back soon, I was going to drive down to the swamp to find them.

Reluctantly, I went into the Pole Bridge, poured a glass of bourbon, and joined the group at the fireplace. The host and huntmaster, a forestry professor named Walter Cabin, was standing with his back to the fire. The others were seated in a semicircle around him, and one of the boys was telling about his hunt. In this same group three years before, John had had to tell of missing a deer. I remembered the hunt—sitting among the long rays of amber light in the waning afternoon and how, after a long time, the appearance of the buck had brought the woods with all its sounds and smells into sudden purpose. John had told of it, sleepy and disconsolate, staring into the fire: "I shot and missed." Helpless to relieve his disappointment, I had been gratified by the response of the men, each of whom had found some way to help John understand that buck fever was no uncommon affliction, at any age.

They were intent now on the story of another boy, apparently unaware that John and Billy had not come in from the swamp. When the boy finished, I said, "I don't know what's keeping John and Billy. Unless they're tracking something."

"They'll be in before long," someone said. "I wouldn't worry about 'em."

"I'm not worried," I said. "I just wonder what's keeping 'em so long."

Walter called on someone else. After a minute or two, I went back outside. The tailgate was down on a pickup. I sat down and settled back, facing south.

John had killed his first deer a few weeks after missing the buck at Groton, but instead of easing his disappointment, it had made things worse.

We had been hunting at Jack Bass's farm north of Athens, sitting at the edge of an open grove of white oaks. It was a cold morning in December, the sun too weak for shadows, and we snuggled against each other for warmth. After a short while I heard a stirring behind us in the thick leaves and turned my head and saw sixty yards away not a buck but a doe, casually eating acorns. I whispered to John, "There's a good doe behind us. I think I'd take her if I were you." We got quietly to our feet behind the cover of the tree. He raised his rifle as I brought my binoculars to my eyes. "Wait a minute," I said. She was not big, but after a second look I decided she was big enough. He looked at me. I nodded and he fired. The doe ran as though she were hit.

The leaves were splashed with red, blatant in the dull light. *Please let us find this deer, and find it soon*, I thought. *And find it dead*. The trail led us to the rusted strands of a barbed-wire fence, strung from one tree to another through the vacant woods. We stood there looking around, wondering if the doe had bellied under the wire. I examined the barbs for hair. John said, "Daddy. There she is," and pointed down the fence row. The doe was on our side, lying in long grass as though she were bedded down, looking at us. She seemed much smaller than she had when standing up. Suddenly I hated everything—the feeble light in the woods, the stubby little forty-four magnum in John's hands, and most of all the next thing I had to do. This was not hunting; it was something else. I was sorry that John was there.

I said, "Stay here," and reached for the rifle, but he followed me anyway. Thirty yards from the deer I raised the rifle and through the scope saw two smooth knobs on the top of the head, the budding antlers of a little buck. I said, "It's a button, son," but I thought *little boy* and cried inside *my God what am I doing to this child*? Then I shot, too quickly, missing the stalk of a neck and gouging a terrible wound in the animal's back. *Just let me finish this quickly and I'll never shoot another deer.* At point-blank range, the deer blurred in the scope.

I dragged the little buck from the woods. John followed along behind. It dragged too easily, and John didn't say anything, intent on plowing the leaves with his boots.

After the deer was dressed and hung, we sat down on the steps of Jack's walk-in cooler. John's natural reticence concealed much of what he was feeling at any time, and on this occasion I couldn't tell whether he was disappointed that his first deer was a half-grown fawn or grieved by its dying. A deer is a deer, I told him, not a person. It is sentimentality that makes a distinction between big deer and little ones. You hate to kill a button because it removes a buck from the herd before he is old enough to reproduce or to become worthy game. But these things happen. In any case, the mistake had been mine, not his. And the venison—what there was of it—would be as tender as lamb or veal. Did he understand?

"Yessir," he said, but he said it in a way that made me want to put my arms around him tight and tell him that he never had to hunt again if he didn't want to. But we were both confused about a lot of things, and something kept me from doing it.

I climbed from the back of the pickup and walked slowly down the road, the white sand of its bed glimmering through the dark woods ahead of me. In a couple of hundred yards it would emerge from the trees and bend again to the south through an open field. From the bend I would be able to see their headlights a long way off.

I wasn't there when Billy had suggested to John that he hunt this afternoon in the swamp, but he had made similar proposals to me so often that I knew exactly how he had done it—abruptly, while John was engaged in some trivial task, like rummaging through his bag for a flashlight— and casually, as though that were the obvious and inevitable choice. Yet also, somehow, with a promise of excitement and adventure. "If you want to kill a buck this afternoon, John, I'd suggest you hunt in the swamp. You can kill a doe off a stand on the hill, but the bucks will be moving in the swamp. That's what I'm going to do. If you want to go with me."

So Billy had seen that John was older than I was treating him and decided, like a good uncle, to take over his training himself. And he was doing it as he had with me, by turning him loose alone.

I stopped in the road. It was not John but I whom Billy was trying to teach. I was the one who had to understand that John would learn what he needed to know only if I were not there to show him. Nor Billy either. As he had chosen not to be with me that day I killed my first buck. It seemed so simple I was surprised I had not seen it before.

I had hardly turned around when I heard the Blazer coming. I stepped off to the right of the road. Directly the beams of the headlights flashed upon me and upon the trees on either side. I turned around to face the blinding glare. Billy eased to a stop beside me. "I thought y'all had decided to spend the night down there," I said.

Billy's smiling voice in the dark, refusing as always to acknowledge the complaint in mine: "Yeah."

"Well, tell me about it. Y'all must have been tracking or dragging, one, to be so late."

"Why don't you just follow us on to the Pole Bridge?"

The cabin was in shouting distance of where we stood. I said, "Thanks just the same but I'll walk," but they were already pulling away by the time I finished the sentence. As they did, I saw in the red glow of the taillight a deer hanging draped across the spare tire on the back. I couldn't see its head, but it looked big enough to be a buck. I began to run, breathless with hope that John was the one who had killed it.

I came up as they were getting out. John broke into a grin—the uncontrollable kind—and I stuck out my hand, meeting his grin with my own. "*All right.* Congratulations. Let's have a look at him. Is it a buck?" Mumbling "Thank you" through his smile, the boy led me to the back of the Blazer. I spotted the head with my flashlight as he lifted it by the antlers. As far as I could tell, the rack was heavy and symmetrical, though a bit shy perhaps of sixteen inches. "That's beautiful, son. How many points?"

"Eight."

"That's beautiful."

Billy stepped forward. "Let's get this gentleman over there in the light so we can get a good look at him."

John and Billy lifted the buck from the tire and lowered it heavily to the ground. Then, grabbing an antler each, they dragged it to a grassy patch in front of the Blazer. As Billy reached into the vehicle to turn on the headlights, the yard filled with people. Leaving John to accept handshakes of congratulations, I went inside to get my camera.

John and Billy and I put off supper to take the buck to the skinning shed. It would take us an hour or more to skin it and hang it in the cooler, but the camp would stay up till we returned. John had a story and Walter Cabin would not let him go to bed until he had told it.

Driving back to the Pole Bridge, I wondered about his performance. John was not much of a talker, especially in front of a group of men. The unembellished fact was all he would have to offer. I was afraid that his plain style might be construed by those who didn't know him well as indifference, a lack of appreciation for the seriousness of killing a deer. The songfeast done well was at once an act of contrition and celebration, a way of coming to terms with the blood one had spilled and an occasion for rejoicing in the opportunity to spill it. Walter Cabin expected the hunter to comport himself as well in the telling as in the hunt itself. I might have coached John if I had had the time, but we were pulling up to the Pole Bridge, and I remembered that it was Billy not I who had taken him to the swamp, where without anyone's assistance he had killed a man's buck.

Everyone was gathered around the fire when we walked in, all of them, well-fed and sleepy, entranced by the play of the flames.

As we were sitting down, Walter spoke in his slow, deliberate way: "John, I believe you have a story to tell."

"There's really not that much to tell," he said, offering—without cue—the standard formula.

"Stand up," Walter said. "If you had killed a spike we'd let you keep your seat, but you'll have to stand up to tell about a buck like that."

So John assumed his place in front of the fire. He had been wet from the waist down since he came in from the swamp. By now he had dried out a little, but his clothes were still damp enough to steam as he backed up to the heat. "I had been sitting under this tree for about an hour," he said.

"Wait a minute," someone interrupted. "Where were you?"

"In L. On Clearwater Stream. My father and I were hunting in that area yesterday and found a heavy crossing where there's some kind of old bridge or something under the water."

He was speaking of an old ford made of logs laid parallel to the flow of the current, the remnant of an ancient logging road long since grown up in forest.

"So I went back there this afternoon."

He stopped and took out a pouch of chewing tobacco, pinched a wad, and stuffed it into his cheek. *Where did that come from?* I wondered.

"Anyway, I didn't see anything for about an hour. It started getting late, and I was worried about walking all the way back in the dark to where Billy was supposed to pick me up. And that's when I saw him. He was coming from the other side. And then he started crossing over to where I was."

"How far were you from the deer, John?" Walter asked.

"Sixty steps. I was going to wait until he came up on my side, but I could see that he was going to come out behind a little rise. So I shot him in the creek."

"Did you have to wade out to get him?" one of the boys asked. John said, "Yeah."

"How deep was it?"

John held his hand palm-down about three feet from the floor. "Not deep. I waded out on that old bridge thing to where he fell and started feeling around under the water." He leaned forward, spreading his arms as though groping for something in the dark. "I felt the antlers," he said, and his hands closed into fists. Then, pantomiming the effort of dragging a wet deer from the creek, he straightened up. "That's about it."

Billy stood up and stepped over to John, extending his right hand and clamping his left around his shoulder. Smiling on behalf of the boy, he turned his handsome face to the group. "He already had him field-dressed when I got there."

They had told me that, but I was pleased for the group to learn that he had undertaken the task alone and in the coming dark, especially when he had known he could count on Billy's help if he waited. I was even more pleased that he hadn't mentioned it himself.

"Don't you think you'd better get out of those wet clothes?" I suggested.

"I'll do it in a minute," he said. "They're almost dry anyway."

I would have welcomed in the telling a word about the beauty of the buck as it had stepped down to the water or the way its antlers had caught the last of the light, but he had done all right. There had been no arrogance, nothing taken for granted. Still, something about his standing in front of the fire in camouflage, telling these men, "So I shot him in the creek," bothered me. Not much, but enough to prompt memory of the child he had been that day on the steps of Jack's cooler, confused but nodding his head because he wanted me to believe he was man enough to deal with what we had done.

I wondered what I had done to him. According to the Eskimo legend, the songfeast saves the hunter, but the legend assumes the necessity of the hunt. Watching John, I wondered if the songfeast would still avail. There was a place beside me on the sofa. I hoped he would come sit down, but Billy took it instead.

"Thanks for taking him today," I said.

"Look-a there," he said.

John was squatting in front of the fire, talking to Walter Cabin and another man. They must have asked him a question because he was tracing with one finger an imaginary map on the floor, and they were paying attention to what he was saying.

"You got a lot to be proud of, pardner," Billy said.

"I know it."

After we had eaten, I went back to the bunkhouse to fetch my pipe. There were no lights in the large room, but I knew almost to the step the distance from the door to my bunk. When I reached it, I knelt down at the foot to find my canvas travel bag. And caught an odor of something wet. John's camouflage outfit—my camouflage—hung before me, suspended dark and long from a nail on the post of the bunk. I had not realized that he had taken it off. I crumpled a damp knee in my fist and caught a whiff of swamp. Getting to my feet, I held the coarse fabric to my face. It smelled of recent exposure—of cypress and oak-leaf mold and faintly but unmistakably of the musk of a rutting buck. Since I had given him the outfit, the responsibility for its odor was mine. But now that he was old enough to fill it out, he would be on his own. Kneeling again for my pipe, I prayed that the fields of his choice might be blessed with the dew of heaven and produce good grain and wine.

10
Fishing Upstream

GROWING UP ON THE EDGE of the low country, I knew nothing of trout and mountain streams. Fishing to me meant sitting—on a warm, shallow pond, in a boat, or on the bank—cane pole and crickets. It was not until I was in my mid-thirties that a friend introduced me to cold-water fishing. By that age, you would think, I should have been sensible enough to keep my wits about me, but I wasn't. From the moment I stepped into running water I knew something was up there, upstream, something other than just fish, and I went after it from one pool to the next like a spawning trout, higher and higher, till streams became brooks, brooks trickles, and afternoons evened into dusk, too dark for me to see. If I had been required to say what that something was, I might have answered, "Winslow Homer," by which I would have meant an experience—not so much of a place as of a moment, a certain light sprayed with the fragrance of hemlock and fern, and a trout jumping in cool blue shadow. That was what I sought each time I went, following the imperious song of an ovenbird, above the noise of the water, further and further upstream.

As I think back over the last ten years, it seems that I spent the first four or five in the riverswamp at Groton standing by the fire with Billy Claypoole and Walter Cabin, Jack Bass and Charlie Creedmore, excited about killing a big buck. Then, as my enthusiasm for deer began to wane, I turned to trout fishing. My impression is that I climbed out of that low-country riverbottom by way of a mountain stream, expecting something that perhaps the swamp had not afforded. But that is not the way it really was. When I check the record I'm surprised to discover that I began trout fishing the same year I joined the Abbot Club. I must have gone to the mountains two or three times a year for several years thereafter, learning a little along the way about casting and flies and running water, before I started talking in my sleep about trout.

Lean, narrow fish, trout hang suspended, poised, in the cold current that shapes them. You can sit on a rock looking into the clear depths with polarized glasses and not see them come, but suddenly they will be there, whether by some trick of light or magic of their own I don't know, but as clean from the hand of God as an acorn.

I was fishing by myself one day, in late afternoon on a creek that was really too small and difficult to fish. By the time the sun went behind the ridge, the stream had narrowed to a canopied stair-case, strewn with boulders and crowded on either side by dense walls of mountain laurel. Pools lay at each level, clear and usually deep enough to hold a few trout, though I would not have ex-pected anything above eight inches, even if I had been able to present a fly. The time came that afternoon when I knew I would have to turn around and start back if I wanted to get to my car by dark, but I kept on, compelled by the lure of headwaters. Gath-ered in the tunnel of the stream, the light of the late afternoon poured down the rocks like water, and the song of an ovenbird—*teacher, teacher, teacher*—rang above the rushing of rapids.

Knowing finally that the next one would have to be the last, I clambered over a boulder and found myself at the brink of a wide, deep pool, too close not to have spooked any fish that might have been there. I didn't care. The pool itself was a catch, something to come upon in that shadowed place, alone, at dusk. Across the pool, on the upstream end, blocking the bed from one side to the other, stood a square wall of damp, mossy rock as big as a cabin. The stream issued from the base of the rock, and also from the rock, a rushing, sucking noise with something in it that sounded almost alive. Anguished.

I ducked behind a boulder and cast at the wall before me. The fly struck the rock and fell to the pool where, like a pinch of milkweed down, it floated nicely, riding high as the flow swept it steadily toward the fissure at the base of the rock. *There is a fish up under there*, I thought, and let it disappear, but directly the fly came dancing out, unmolested. I retrieved it and cast again, almost a reflex action; again nothing hit it. When I retrieved it that time I reeled the line in all the way; the snag of the fly in the tip guide said *quit* and I waded from the pool.

The rock moaned. As late as it was I wanted to see about that sound so I climbed the steep hillside on the right, pulling myself up through a tangle of laurel branches, trailing my rod behind. Emerging from the thicket at the top, I could see that the rock was like a slab, standing on end and leaning against a huge monolith that shouldered out of the hill. The channel of the stream, instead of seeking a way around that shoulder, slid across it for a short distance; then, funnelled into a tight curve, it plunged in a roaring spout down through the crevice between the slab and the shoulder. I crawled across a mat of wet leaves to see. The spin of the twisting spout had carved a spiral chimney in the space between the rocks. I could see no pool below but knew there had to be one and, in its perpetual darkness, a monster of a trout.

I sat back on the wet rock and stuffed my pipe, wondering how it would be to drop a fly down that furious torrent. In the creamy seethe at the bottom the fly would appear like a mote of battered

insect for less than a second. No fish was that quick. Even if one
could snatch it I would never be able to draw it up against the
smashing force of the spout. I lit my pipe and listened to the
water. Its sounds had filled my afternoon so that I had long since
stopped hearing it, but now as I tried to listen, I began to hear,
beneath the incessant roar of the spout through the crevice, bab-
blings and splashings and quiet little garglings, a variety of small
hydraulic sounds, and now and then, erratically, as though the
rock had a mind of its own, the anguished sucking from deep inside. Living water, Jesus said, cold and splashing as from a mountain stream. *Water alive with fish*, I thought, *teeming with trout*.

When I knocked the ashes from my pipe it was dark enough for
me to see the sparks. I descended the hill on the other side of the
rock. Almost at the bottom, my heels dug into wet, leafy soil. My
left hand clutching an outcropping of stone, I noticed a hole in the
rock, an orifice with jagged edges maybe a foot and a half in di-
ameter. In cross-section the stone was not solid, but like a shell
scooped concave from underneath by the torque of swirling water.

That must have happened during times of flood. The pool below was quiet now, its surface perhaps six feet beneath the hole
lapping in concentric rings, dancing in the dark, in the midst of
the living rock.

Holding the leader carefully, I lowered the fly through the hole
onto the pool.

The fly was an Adams. The fish must have seen it coming. Just
as the fly touched the surface, the fish rose from the darkness,
whitish, and arced at the top of the water in a dull flash. The
leader bit into my palm. It was a strong fish. I hauled it up without

finesse or ceremony, fell back against the rock, away from the hole, and held it dangling at arm's length. It was a rainbow, not a monster but a wild trout and bigger than any I had ever caught. I imagined, more than saw, the rose stripe along its flank.

I reached for it but stopped, even as my hand was about to grasp it. What good was one fish? Hardly enough for a meal unless I planned to eat alone. I didn't want to do that. Not with trout. For a supper of fresh trout I would want Billy and Walter Cabin, the three of us camped by the pool below, and maybe Jack Bass if he could manage to climb this far, and if Jack, Charlie Creedmore too; the five of us and any stranger who might find comfort in our circle, on a night cool enough for the fire to draw the circle close; and on the fire, trout in a skillet, battered and frying in butter, enough for us all.

I made my way to the edge of the pool. Against such a time as that, I lowered the fish into the water. Holding it in a swimming position, I freed the fly from its mouth. The fish lay still. When I opened my hand, it listed a little to one side so I moved it back and forth, gently, while the stream through the rock rushed and moaned; then a tremor, a tiny spasm, one strong kick, and the trout was gone.

J ACK BASS MUST HAVE loved big water. Although his farm had an excellent fish pond on it as well as a beaver swamp where wood ducks and mallards roosted, he would often choose to go fishing or duck hunting on one of the big hydroelectric power lakes that lay along the Savannah River sixty miles away. That might have been understandable if he had been consistently successful, but more often than not he returned with an empty game bag.

I know that the quality of a fishing or hunting trip is determined by more important things than meat in the pot, but the big lakes, as far as I was concerned, were as boring as mud puddles, bleak in the winter, wide open and hot in the summer. But Jack didn't care. At the peak of our brief duck season, when hundreds of mallards and even a few black ducks had replaced the woodies on the roost ponds at his farm, Jack would call his brother Gene or his number-one hunting buddy Charlie Creedmore: "Y'all want to go to Clark's Hill Friday?" That would begin a week of preparations—buying food (to be cooked on a grill in the boat), rigging decoys (two hundred hand-carved pintails), packing camouflage netting (the kind used by the Army to conceal gun emplacements), and assembling the pipe superstructure that would convert the boat into a floating blind. All of this, as well as driving for hours in the dark, by car and boat, to spend a long, cold, sometimes rainy Saturday on the big water, scanning the sky with aching necks for ducks that were always too wary to call. After spending the night in a cheap motel, they would come limping in on Sunday, hungover and tired, raving about what a good time they'd had; couldn't wait to do it again.

"Why?" I asked Charlie Creedmore. "When he could kill all

the big ducks he wants up at the farm, without freezing to death in the process."

"When you get Jack Bass figured out," he said, "you be sure and let me know. I've been going with that sucker for almost ten years and I ain't figured it out yet."

Even so, I thought Jack meant the pond at the farm when he called one night in July to ask me to go fishing with him the next day. For one thing, the next day was Tuesday, and Jack was always in his office during the week, or out on a construction site. He often complained, in fact, that the pressures of his business left too little time for hunting and fishing. "He must be thinking about a quick trip to the farm," I figured. "Two hours at daylight and back in town by eight." That suited me. The pond at Jack's farm was deep and cold and full of big bluegills. Three governors had fished there as well as a nationally known entertainer and one president of the United States. And invitations were few and far between. Jack had inherited the farm from his father and along with it his father's proprietary attitude. Not that he wasn't generous. He liked nothing better, in fact, than playing the role of host. On a dove shoot, for example, Jack would spend the afternoon driving around the field with a big cooler of soft drinks in the back of his pickup, and when the shoot was over and the sweaty hunters were sitting around on the tailgates of their trucks counting out birds, Jack would make a ceremony of opening a cooler of beer and passing around the icy bottles.

Though Jack had told me that I was welcome to fish at the farm whenever I wanted, as long as I picked up a permission slip from his office, I had learned quickly not to take the pond for granted;

to do so deprived him of the pleasure of inviting you himself. It was better to wait for him to do the asking, but invitations, as I have said, were few and far between.

I said, "Yeah, I sure would."

"Good. Be at my house at five o'clock in the morning. We're going to Clark's Hill."

Oh Lord, I groaned. *That means an all-day trip.*

"Okay. What do I need to bring," I asked, wondering what I *could* bring. Clark's Hill was bass water, the kind of place where professional anglers fish for money. My tackle consisted of two fly rods and two ultralight spinning rods. I didn't mind catching a bass with light tackle on a farm pond, if one fairly came my way, but I had never fished for them on purpose.

"Just bring yourself," Jack said. "I got everything we need."

"What about food?"

"I got everything."

I was afraid of that too. As far as Jack was concerned, a good fisherman's lunch was sardines in mustard sauce, Vienna sausages and soda crackers, and maybe a can of Castleberry's butterscotch pudding for dessert.

"You be at my house at five o'clock now."

I said I would.

Jack lived in a Williamsburg-style brick house on the most prestigious street in town. A light was burning in the kitchen when I turned into his drive. Finding myself face to face with his Blazer, I pulled off into a parking area beneath three tall pines and got out. To avoid waking anyone, I went around to the kitchen. As soon as I opened the door the family Pekingese attacked, growling ludicrously, and went to work on the cuff of my trousers. Trying to snatch my cuff from the dog's teeth, I kicked as high as I could, but the dog held on. Jack grabbed it out of mid-air.

"You little Bowser sonofabitch," he said and, stepping to the door, tossed the dog onto the top of a boxwood hedge.

"Did he get you, Jim?"

"Just my pants leg."

Jack was laughing. "I was hoping he had bit you. I'm just waiting for an excuse to get rid of him."

Jack opened the refrigerator and took out a quart of buttermilk. "You want some buttermilk, Jim?"

I said no thank you, I'd never learned to like it.

"You get an ulcer you'll drink it. Whether you like it or not. Doctor told me to drink a quart a day."

Jack turned up the carton and drank, his throat working as he gulped down the milk. When he had finished, he wiped away a thick moustache with the back of his hand and said, "Aaah. I always liked it though." Then he took the lid from a pot on the stove and fished out a plug of link sausage; it was caked with grease from last night's supper.

"Sausage?"

I said no thank you, I'd eaten a bowl of cereal before I left.

"I'm ready if you are," he said.

We drove east across three counties with the stereo turned up high. As the sun rose in our faces, George Jones and Merle Haggard were singing about some bums in Chicago:

> A bearded man in an army coat
>   Said, "The answer, boys, is Jesus."

But one called Joe said, "All I know,
    Ain't January hell?"

Jack laughed at those lines and said they were both right. I said it
was a good song.

When we got to the lake, Jack backed onto the ramp and we
climbed out to transfer gear from the Blazer to the boat. The boat
was a sixteen-foot flatbottom with a seventy-horse motor, big like
everything else Jack owned. The cooler was big, an Igloo that took
both of us to hoist over the side of the boat; the tackle box was
heavy too, a complicated affair of trays and drawers that held
enough tackle for ten men; and he had brought six rods. When
everything was loaded, I stood back and watched Jack back the
trailer down the ramp. I was standing barefoot in the shallows.
The red mud that squished between my toes was cold, but I could
tell already that it was going to be a hot day. The sun through the
haze was a copper coin but it was gaining strength, and the water
was perfectly still, unrippled by any breath.

All day, I thought. *He said we were going to fish all day.*

Jack headed into the sun. I closed my eyes against the wind and
the glare and settled back into the steady drone of the motor. It
felt as though we were skidding and bouncing over a hard surface,
whap, whap, *whap*. From time to time I opened my eyes, but the
landscape offered only the pine-green woods and the raw, red-
clay ribbon of shoreline.

When Jack stopped we were in a wide, shallow bay, the far end
of which was banked with red dirt, and the bank was bolstered
by a jumble of broken granite rock. It was an ugly place to fish.

"You been paying attention, Jim?"

"To what?"

"To how we came in. What if something happened to me, and you had to get us out?"

"Well, I'll tell you like John told me one time, since I didn't, you better not let anything happen to you."

Jack handed me a rod with a closed-face Zebco reel. The lure was already tied on, a green and silver, jointed Mirro-lure, a-dangle with treble hooks.

"Three years ago, I think it was," I said. "John must have been about eleven. We were down at Groton, hunting back in there behind Dead Lake one afternoon, and John shot a pig. If he hadn't been so excited about it, I wouldn't have let him shoot it—it was getting so late, and you know what a hell of a drag that is."

Jack interrupted, "I figured that out a long time ago: if you hunt close to the road you'll kill game close to the road."

"Well, we weren't close to any road that night. Anyway, I told John, 'Lead the way, son, I'll do the dragging.' He couldn't have looked more stunned if I had told him to swim the Savannah River. I didn't have the heart to really make him do it, and besides that it was getting dark fast, so I just told him the same thing you said, 'What if something happened to me and you *had* to get us out?' And that's when he said, 'You better not let anything happen to you then.' Which is exactly the case right now."

Jack laughed and cast toward the granite bank. "I did the same thing with Bubba down there when he was about that age. It's good for them boys to learn that we ain't always going to be around to show them how to do things."

I had heard Jack say that kind of thing a couple of times lately, just enough to bother me a little. "I guess so."

After ten minutes of fruitless casting Jack said, almost apologetically, "We tore 'em up in here back in the spring. On the Fresh Sign trip."

He was referring to a sportsman's club founded years before by his father. From what I had heard it was a large, rather loose group of local businessmen who went to the mountains once a year to hunt deer and to one of the big lakes in the spring to fish. I had gathered also that only a handful actually did much hunting and fishing.

One year, Jack had told me, the group arrived at the Wildlife Management Area in the mountains to find the gate locked. National Forest officials, it seemed, had postponed opening day of deer season by twenty-four hours. "And there we were. Fourteen pickups and an eight-ton stake-body truck loaded with a cord of firewood, fifty chickens, and a barbeque grill. Nowhere to go and it too hot for them chickens to keep. I told everybody to sit tight, and me and Creedmore drove down to Helen. That was before they tried to glamorize it with all that Swiss Alps shit—it used to be a beautiful little town. Anyway, we found a motel called the Chattahoochee Inn. I walked in the lobby, asked this woman behind the desk, 'You got any vacancies?' 'Yes sir,' she said, 'I've got twenty-six.' I said 'I'll take 'em.' You should have seen her face. 'And one more thing,' I said. 'We got fifty chickens need barbecuing tonight. We brought our own grill and charcoal; all we need is the parking lot to cook 'em in.' She said, 'Sir, you have just rented the moe-tel. The parking lot comes with it. You can do anything out there you want to.'

"The Auburn game was on teevee that night. By the time we got the grill going people were starting to get lickered up pretty good, and when the game came on they opened every damn door of that motel and turned the teevees up wide open. You could have heard 'em in Athens. Ain't no telling how many wrecks we caused."

That was typical of the stories I had heard about the Fresh Sign Club so I said to Jack, "I didn't know y'all actually did any fishing on the Fresh Sign weekend."

"Oh hell yeah," he said. "Me and Creedmore caught a coolerful of bass right in here along this bank."

"You must have caught them all, then, because there sure as hell ain't any in here now," I said.

Once or twice during the next hour Jack jerked his rod back and said "Ho now!" but that was as close as either of us came to catching a fish. By ten o'clock the sun was dancing brightly on the water. Sweat was stinging my eyes. I locked my face into a squint and held it against the glare.

"You reckon we could have just as much fun if we moved up the lake a piece?" Jack asked.

I couldn't see that moving would improve the fishing because the whole lake seemed empty to me, devoid not only of fish but of anything congenial to the spirit or even pleasing to the eye. But I was ready to get out of the sun. "Let's see if we can find some shade," I suggested.

We moved several times that morning, but each new spot was as dead as the one before. For a while we fished in the shady lee of a small island. I would have been content to stay there, fish or no fish, but Jack seemed impervious to the sun. His face had turned beet-red, but he just tied a bandanna around his head to keep the sweat from running into his eyes and kept on casting. Once he said, "It's hot ain't it." I tried to make him out, but he shimmered in the glare, dark and out of focus. For the twentieth time that morning I said, "I don't believe they're going to bite, Jack."

"What's the matter, Jim? You not having fun?"

"Not as much as I could be if we were up at the farm," I answered, a little surprised at myself, even as I spoke, but too blind and hot to care what effect the statement might have on Jack.

It had none, apparently. "You ready to eat?" he asked.

At that point even sardines in mustard sauce sounded good. It occurred to me, in fact, that the only way a civilized person could eat such food was to be stuck in a bass boat on big water, with the sun beating down.

Jack took a grocery sack from the cooler and from the sack a big red and white paper bucket. "Hope you like chicken, Jim, 'cause that's all we got."

I reached for a drumstick, noting sure enough that the bucket contained nothing else, no rolls, slaw, or potato salad. But the chicken tasted good, and I said so. Jack said it was all right for fast food, but for flavor it couldn't touch a yard bird. "You ever eat yard chicken for Sunday dinner?" he asked. I said I remembered my grandmother's cook wringing a chicken's neck and how fascinated I had been by the horror of the headless bird's crazy running, pumping blood.

"That's how my daddy got started in the poultry-packing business," Jack said.

I had heard that Mr. Bass had made his fortune in chickens, but I had never heard the details.

"Yard chickens," he said. "That's how he got started. Him and this colored fellow named Earl used to drive all over northeast Georgia—Oglethorpe, Barrow, Banks, Oconee, Madison, Jackson and Wilkes—buying chickens. Every pullet he could find.

Then we'd dress 'em at the house. My mother and Earl's wife and me. I wasn't but about ten years old. Down there on Hancock Street. We picked chickens all day long. And hot! You couldn't run a fan because of the feathers, see. And the whole house smelled like scalded chicken. It just kind of settled into the drapes and rugs. Ain't nothing in the world smells like scalded chicken feathers."

"It's a wonder to me that you can still eat it," I said.

"What? Chicken? I love it. Have another piece."

"Thanks. How did he market them?"

"Packed 'em in boxes and took 'em around to the grocery stores—A&P, Winn-Dixie, a lot of little stores. Used to be, if you bought a chicken from the A&P, it was somebody's homegrown yard bird."

"How did he get from that house on Hancock Street to all those plants I've heard of?"

"He bought him a conveyor belt and assembly-lined the poultry-packing business. The way you dressed chickens, see, you had to cut them on both sides of the neck—vein and artery—and bleed 'em out. Government made you do it that way. The old man invented this W-shaped rack to hang chickens on two at a time, and then he staggered right-handed people with left-handed people down both sides of the table. Hired everybody in my mother's family and his too. Hell, he was delivering chickens twice as fast as everybody else. Did it all in ten years and then sold out. You ready for another piece?"

Jack extended the bucket to me. I was surprised to see that it was already half empty. I had had only two pieces; by the bones floating around the boat I figured he had eaten three to my one.

"Why did he sell out?" I asked.

"That's just the way he was. When he decided to do something, he went ahead and did it, and he didn't worry about trying to explain it. You just had to know him."

So the farm wasn't all Jack inherited from his father.

Just then the light changed, the harsh glare dimmed into plain daylight and the impact of the sun abated. I looked over my shoulder. A storm cloud loomed above us as deep and angry as a bruise; its rolling upper edge was aglow with gold, and beams like the points of a crown radiated from it.

Because he was facing me, I realized, Jack must have been aware of the darkening sky for some time before the cloud covered the sun. Yet he had not mentioned it.

Turning back, I saw Jack clearly for the first time since we had been on the water. His cheeks were shiny with chicken, and in his countenance was a deep contentment.

It wasn't to catch fish at all, I realized, that he had come fishing today.

"We're going to get some weather out of that," I said. "Any minute now."

"Looks like it," he said, but he made no move to leave.

"We better get out of here before it hits, don't you think?"

"You worried about getting wet, Jim?"

"No, I'm worried about how I'm going to get us back if you get struck by lightning."

Jack laughed. "If I get struck by lightning, you won't have to worry about getting us back. 'Cause like the man said, we're in the same boat, brother."

"I don't know, Jack. Billy had two guys working for him down at Brunswick last summer—in a boat out in the marsh—and lightning hit them out of a clear blue sky. One of them—a guy named Charles—picked himself up out of the bottom of the boat, but his buddy was nowhere to be seen. Then he saw something red floating in the water a little way off and remembered that Todd had been wearing a red shirt. He managed to get him back in the boat and gave him CPR, even though he thought Todd was dead—his hair and beard were completely singed off and his belt was welded to his zipper. The motor *was* dead so Charles got out and pulled the boat all the way in to the marina. Cut his feet to ribbons on the oyster beds, but the doctor said he saved Todd's life."

Jack laughed again. "Well, you won't have to worry about no oyster beds if you have to haul me in. That's one thing for damn sure." With that he gave the rope a pull. The motor caught and Jack swung it around, opening the throttle all the way. The boat stood up, dug in and shot forward, straight toward the clear blue sky over Georgia.

12
Amazing Grace

JACK BASS CAME HOME FROM a banquet one hot night in late August and cleaned his shotguns. He must have been thinking about dove season, trying to decide perhaps whom to invite to the opening-day shoot at his farm. He always waited until the last minute, when those of us who expected invitations began to get a little nervous, knowing that Jack liked to keep it small, twenty guns or so, and that there was almost no one he felt obligated to ask.

They found his over-and-under the next morning on the table where he'd left it, still broken down, as though he had been interrupted in the middle of cleaning it.

Jane awakened me at seven o'clock. Telephone, she said. I stumbled into the kitchen and took the receiver.

"Jim?" It was a familiar voice, but I was to sleepy to place it.

"Yes."

"It's about Jack."

"All right."

"Jack Bass. He died last night."

People say that such news often takes a moment or two to sink in, but I had not had time to generate the protective atmosphere that gets us safely through a day, so I just sat down on the floor and wept.

Jack loved all the old camp-meeting songs, but his favorite was "Amazing Grace." They sang it at the funeral, the sanctuary full and on its feet, latecomers standing in the vestibule and a good many even in the yard. I figured if I could make it through the hymn I'd be all right.

that saved a wretch like me.

Nobody would have called Jack a wretch; he laughed too much for that. But he used to belt out that line like he meant it. At church one Sunday night, when they announced "Amazing Grace," he had turned and smiled back at me, knowing I loved it too. Then, seeing that I was alone as he was, he had beckoned me to come down and join him. We were just getting to that part about the wretch when I eased into the pew beside him; he had put his heavy arm around my shoulder, singing at the top of his voice.

> *I once was lost but now am found,*
> *Was blind but now I see.*

Those of us who were pallbearers stood in a row in the front pew, most of us members of the Abbot Club. Two or three were having trouble controlling themselves; I was concerned about my own composure.

> *When we've been there ten thousand years*
> *Bright shining as the sun . . .*

I went up to Jack's farm after the funeral. I'd thought I might do a little fishing. It had been hot at the cemetery, but the evening was growing cool by the time I got to the pond, August burning low, as Emily Dickinson puts it. The sun was a red ball in a grainy sky, the foliage around the pond frayed and dull.

Two boats rocked gently in their berths in the boathouse, cobwebbed in the corners as though they had not been used all summer. That was not true, of course; I had fished in one of them in July, though I couldn't tell which one—not that it mattered. Both were metal, big and wide, unwieldy as bathtubs; and the rear seats in both, where Jack was used to sitting, were badly bent in the middle. Electric motors were fixed to the sterns, but the only battery I saw was dead so I looked around until I found a paddle. The blade was broken, but I could manage with it. For no particular reason, I chose the boat on the right.

A breeze took me as soon as I cleared the berth, a steady breeze angling across the water from the east, flaking the surface with light. I opened the rod case and removed the red satin sleeve, untied it and pulled it back from the glistening sections of graphite rod. The wind was blowing me back toward the boathouse so I laid the rod aside and paddled toward the middle of the pond. Then I returned to the rod, fitting one section into the socket of the other. As I opened the reel case, the wind pushed me back again, and the boat struck the dock that ran along the front of the house. I said to hell with the fly rod and began paddling hard, headed across the wind toward a deep cove in the corner of the pond. Bream had bedded there in May and June. Though bedding was over for this summer, the water was smooth and dark, protected by the wooded bank. As I fought against the wind, I kept sliding down the seat into the crease in the center; from there the paddle barely reached the water on either side.

I looked back at the house to see how far I had come. It was easy to imagine Jack on the dock, leaning against the rail as he had been that evening last month, his back to me on the water as he talked and laughed with Charlie Creedmore. I had been fishing along the dam that afternoon. Billy had been expected but had not arrived, and Jack and Charlie had thought it was too hot for the fish to bite so I had been in the boat by myself. In spite of the warning rumbles of an approaching storm I had waited too late to leave, wanting to try one more time to sidearm the popping bug in under the myrtles, to the undisturbed shadows where big bream lay. I had never caught one, not the kind Jack called a tittie bream, a country term for a fish so big that instead of gripping it with your hand you have to hold it against your chest to get the hook out. I had been trying so hard that afternoon that I had ignored the storm until a loud crash of thunder sent me hurrying across the water.

I had swung the boat into a rising wind, switching the electric motor to full throttle, but the wind offset its feeble push, stopping me in place. I was frightened and felt silly, aware of myself leaning frantically into the wind, one hand on the throttle, as though I were someone else, attempting a heroic life-saving mission without knowing that he wasn't getting anywhere. But I knew it, and knew that the boat was metal and that the life I was trying to save was my own. The lightning unnerved me, quick forks incandescent against the dark cloud, and I realized that each conscious moment might be my last. I'd never know what hit me. All the while I could see Jack and Charlie. They seemed to be telling jokes because now and then I caught snatches of easy laughter, and once a whiff of steaks on the grill.

When I was halfway across, the whole pond held its breath and flickered, as though the particles of dust in the air were about to ignite. Then in a thundering crash they did, blinding me so that I feared I was dead. When the last echoes of thunder died away, I heard Jack's laughter again and looked up to see him still against the rail, indifferent to my plight. I was furious, almost to the point of tears. *How could he not know,* I thought, *that I might never make it in?* And I longed for him to turn, if only to share my terror. But not until I reached the boathouse did I see his face. As I was nosing the boat into its berth, he came over to the steps, grinning: "Better have a beer, Jim. You look kind of nervous."

I entered the cove, crossing the line between ripply water and smooth, and reached again for my reel.

I could still see his back, as broad as a bale of cotton, but I couldn't get him to turn his face any more than I had been able to that afternoon in July.

I screwed on the reel and stripped off leader. Sometimes in my haste to fish I would tie on a popping bug before threading the line through the guides, but I was deliberate this time, almost afraid that I might go to pieces if I made such a mistake. Carefully, I took a new bug from its packet, a chartreuse one, and scraped the enamel paint from the eye of the hook with my knife. Then I tied it on with an improved clinch, wetting the knot with my mouth before I pulled it snug. The boat sat still on the water, close enough to the bank for me to reach it with a cast but not too close. The woods around the pond were abuzz with insects, cicadas I supposed: I could hear no birds above their incessant sawing, but now and then a swallow swooped and dipped in the deepening haze.

If I could just have seen his face, not as in a photograph, merely remembered, but alive and looking at me, I might have been able to start fishing. Instead, I sat, witless as the insects, unwilling to make the first cast. It was not some assurance that Jack was still alive that I was after, but a sense of Jack himself. He seemed to be going away from me, constantly disappearing into the haze of early September, and I just wanted him to turn around so I could see his face again.

With an effort I raised the rod. The popping bug struck the grassy bank, bounced off and plopped onto the water, making little circles. I let it sit for a full minute. Then I gave it a twitch or two and cast again. I was surprised that nothing hit it. With my left hand I took the paddle and made one stroke further along the bank. I cast again, right against the edge, and again the popping bug sat undisturbed. Its yellow glow in the dark green shadows pleased me. I didn't care whether I caught a fish or not.

With one such cast after another, increasingly mechanical, I moved deeper into the cove. The cove became a cave with a leafy roof, forcing me to roll cast. The deeper I went, the darker it got. After a while I began to think of going in, but when I looked back toward the mouth of the cove, the open water beyond sparkled as bright as mid-afternoon. No hurry.

A mountain stream is different, I thought. The last time I had been trout fishing I had stayed on the stream too late. Enraptured by the way falling water spilled forth light from down between the walls of mountain laurel, I had kept on fishing, climbing from pool to pool as the woods grew dark around me. The trip back down the mountain had been a long, rough stumble. *That's the trouble with rivers. You never know how far they're going to take you. On a pond like this you just fish around the edges until you get back to where you started. If it begins to get dark before you finish, you go on in because there is nothing out here to hold you unless the fish are biting. Even then you have nothing to worry about because you are secured by surrounding bank. A river is a road and a mountain stream a stairway, but any pond is home compared to running water.*

Unless the pond is as big as Clark's Hill Lake and the darkness a white fog as blind as any night you ever stumbled through.

We had been duck hunting on Clark's Hill a couple of winters back, Jack's brother Gene and I in one blind, Jack and Charlie Creedmore out on a point two hundred yards away. It was midmorning, the sky empty as it had been since daylight, the water gray and choppy. Just as I was beginning to realize that I could no longer see the outermost decoys, Jack came walking over from his blind and announced that it was time to get the hell out of there if we didn't want to get socked in. The marina was three miles away, "and we don't want to end up like them boys they was looking for yesterday," he said, referring to two hunters who had drowned on the lake the week before.

We were in two boats. Jack and Charlie led the way, and we followed close in their churning wake. As the air grew visible and dense, it blotted out the smudge of distant shoreline, the fields of gray water on either side, and finally even Jack sometimes, depending on how far he surged ahead. We rode for a long time that way, I conscious of nothing but his broad back. Then, abruptly, Jack shut off his motor and swung aside, pulling us behind him. A dark wall of pines stood before us. We would have to turn one way or the other, but the brothers disagreed on the right direction. Gene was convinced that a narrow passage between two islands lay to our right; Jack was in no mood to argue. "All right, Gene. Y'all go ahead. We'll wait right here. Let us know when you find it now."

In ten minutes we were lost, enveloped by a cloud so dense we seemed to be not merely in it but afloat upon its buoyance, suspended. I could make out my hand before my face, but Gene in the stern was a dim blur, like an image outlined in chalk on a smudged chalkboard. He yelled to me above the steady *putt-putt-putt* of the motor to be on the lookout for stumps and snags.

Oh Lord. I hadn't thought of that. Leaning forward in the bow, I realized that I could not see far enough ahead to shout a warning in time for him to stop. The possibility began to bother me. Soon I was imagining dead trees drifting in the silence before us.

"Slow down!" I yelled.

Gene cut the motor off. The boat heaved forward and stopped, pitching from its own momentum. "What's the matter? You see a stump?"

"No. You were going too fast. Let's sit still a minute. We might hear their motor."

"They're probably listening for ours."

"Let's be quiet."

But there was only the slapping of waves against the hull.

"Holler," Gene said.

Good idea, I thought. But I couldn't do it. If no one answered back, I feared, the silence would be unbearable.

"Hooooeeeeeeeeeeee," Gene called, a high, quavering inquisitive plea that offended the white stillness like giggling in a cathedral. As the whoop tailed off, the fog seemed to thicken.

"This ain't worth a damn," he said.

I said I knew it.

I don't know how long we sat there. One loses a sense of time in a situation like that; with no form or color to engage the eye one begins after a while to retreat into a shell of paralyzed sensation. Had it not been for the cold and the dizzying smell of gasoline I might have thought I had died.

"Jim. Listen."

I could hear nothing.

"Hear it?"

"No."

"Listen."

Yes. Something. It might have been a whoop. I couldn't tell. Gene grinned: "That's them." And whooped back. Directly we heard from far off the sputtering cough of an outboard motor starting up and then the snarl and steady whine. Somebody was coming.

The sound of the motor grew louder. Soon it seemed so close that I began to fear they might run over us in the fog. The sound became a roar. When they were almost on top of us, the noise suddenly stopped and our boat began to rock with the waves of their wake. A paddle struck the side of their boat, and I could hear the slosh of water.

"Whooee," they called, softly.

Gene and I both answered.

Then Jack's voice, clear and unmistakable: "You boys find what you were looking for?"

A blur appeared in the fog, assumed color and definition, grew large. Charlie Creedmore went floating by, a paddle's length away, and then as the stern of their boat swung toward us, Jack's face, as deep as oxblood through the drifting mist.

I had never felt so found in my life.

As I sat on the pond that evening, I remembered that Jack had extended a cigarette lighter toward me, igniting it out of the fog. I recalled the fire and the big hand that held it, but his face, just beyond arm's reach, refused to come into focus. The fog in my memory merged with the grainy haze of the buzzing summer twilight, but the face remained unfeatured, gauzy red. I knew the time had come for me to go.

Most fisherman make at least one cast after they decide to quit.

I was out of the cove, halfway back to the boathouse. Light lingered on the pond, but the woods were dark. I made a perfunctory cast and a fish hit the popping bug almost before the bug hit the water. It was a strong fish, a bass I thought at first, but it ran like a bluegill, in a straight line to deep water. When I tried to pull it in, it fought harder than any bream I'd ever felt, bowing the graphite rod into a horseshoe. I let it run. When it tired, I brought it alongside and reached for the taut leader, hoping the fish would not flip free as I lifted it from the water. Safe in the boat, hanging rigid from the line, it was bigger even than I had expected, maybe as much as a pound; and the irridescent blue edging on its gills, catching what light was left, shone like neon. I reached for the fish, meaning to flatten its spiny dorsal fin as I grabbed it, but my hand was not big enough for a firm grip. So I clapped it to my chest and began to work at the hook. This was a tittie bream if there ever was one.

At that I turned toward the dock, maybe even a second before I heard the familiar sound of his red-clay voice. And there he was: the red bandanna tied around his head, the scant wisps of yellow hair looking glued to his scalp, the full lips grinning: "What you got, Jim, a tittie bream?"

I smiled as the hook came free and said, aloud but softly, "Yeah."

I returned the fish to the pond, holding it upright until it recovered its equilibrium. It stood for five seconds perhaps between my palms and then with one hard ripple of its body it was gone, instantly, out of sight in the deep, dark water.

13
Peace in the Valley

Jack Bass used to sing "Peace in the Valley." In front of the fire at the Pole Bridge, after supper, a red bandanna tied around his head, he'd take his guitar and run through his repertoire: "Amazing Grace," "Just a Closer Walk," "Peace in the Valley." I was always struck by the irony of his singing that song:

> And the beasts of the wild
> Will be led by a child
> And there will be peace
> Peace in the valley . . .

Next morning the valley of the Savannah River would ring with the shots of high-powered rifles, and some of the shots would be his and every now and then some would be mine.

The song is based on the famous passage in Isaiah 11, in which the prophet envisions the Day of the Lord and describes it in terms of amicable relations among all creatures: the wolf and the lamb, the leopard and the kid, the lion and the calf; a little child shall lead them, and none shall hurt nor destroy in all My holy mountain.

But fall continues to come to the Savannah River Swamp. In obedience to their own imperatives, red-shouldered hawks take squirrels, bobcats take young pigs, otters an occasional wood duck, and in the tall grass on the edge of the hill, big canebrake rattlers buzz at the sound of approaching feet—the old dispensation, Yahweh to Noah after the Flood:

> And the fear of you and the terror of you
> shall be on every beast of the earth and on
> every bird of the sky; with everything that creeps

on the ground, and all the fish of the sea,
into your hand they are given.

During the years that I have been hunting at Groton, seven members of the club have been divorced, four have changed professions, three have dropped out, and Jack Bass is dead, but the Savannah River Swamp remains the same, observing the changing light from one season to the next, year after year. With the conclusion of each hunting season I wonder if I will go again, for I think I have noticed lately a growing disaffection for killing deer. But I was back again this year to watch the reluctant summer give way to autumn, and to smell once more the stirring musk of a rutting buck. Whether or not I really want to kill the buck, I am not yet willing to forego the company of men who hunt. So I take some comfort in the old dispensation and tell myself that what we have between now and the coming of the Day of the Lord is riverswamps.

Saturday of last year's November weekend:
Billy dropped me off in the swamp at first light. I whispered good luck to him and the guest who was hunting with him and quietly loaded my rifle as the Blazer pulled away. Then I started through the woods toward Clearwater Stream, looking for a particular grove of oaks where I had killed three deer in past years.

I approached it this time with little expectation of success. A promised cold front had stalled, it seemed, and the weather was too warm for November, too warm for hunting. The sky looked dirty, and I could feel on the back of my neck a muggy breathing out of the east. I circled the grove and came into it from the stream side so that I could face the hill with the grove in front of me. Deer are not likely to move much on a day like that. If they were stirring at all, I figured, it would be in a routine early drift from the hill into the swamp. I settled between the flaring roots of an oak and laid my rifle across my lap.

When the light had come as fully as the clouds would allow, leaves began to fall, a heavy shower throughout the swamp, as far in all directions as I could hear.

I tried to focus my attention on the walls of cane that fenced the grove, but I was distracted for no good reason by the memory of a woman I had known many years before. I wondered what had become of her.

It seemed appropriate that I had come into the swamp this morning with Billy. Had it not been for him I would probably have given up hunting ten years before. He had led me into the woods again, into deeper woods than I had ever known, to the beaver swamps along the Oconee and Appalachee, into the Abbot Club and so to this very riverbottom. We had driven through the swamp this morning without headlights because Billy loved the vagueness of the woods at first light; we had driven slowly, though not so slowly as to keep from spilling coffee, down the road that ran beside Clearwater Stream, past the Big Oak that Jack Bass had loved.

During the September hunt after Jack's death someone had nailed a red bandanna to the tree. I had always suspected Charlie Creedmore. Three years had passed since then. The last time I'd seen the bandanna, back in October, it had faded to the neutral tone of the trunk, but I had noticed this morning that a new one hung in its place, as dark as a splash of blood against the gray. I had not been able to tell whether Billy saw it or not. He could be peculiar about such things as bandannas nailed to trees in the swamp. So I had observed the new one in silence as we drove past.

Billy had had trouble with Jack at first. Because he was often coarse and boisterous, Billy had decided, he must also be insensitive to the swamp. Jack of course had laughed at Billy's resentment; if Billy couldn't take a joke, screw him. Though I had soon grown to love Jack, I had not understood his role in the club until I learned that some aborigine hunting parties in Australia consist of four defined specialists: the leader or huntmaster, the shaman who prays for success and sometimes envisions the location of game, the spearman-tracker, and the fool. The function of the fool is to make the others laugh, even at themselves, lest they take their own roles too seriously and spoil the hunt. In order to do that he must be willing at times to make a fool of himself. I doubted that Jack was fully conscious of performing that function in the Abbot Club, but the effect was the same. When I mentioned that to a friend who had hunted as a guest at the Pole Bridge, he suggested another advantage: when you see what a two-seventy does to the muscle tissue of an animal as big as you are, he said, you have to be blind and stupid too not to realize your own vulnerability; what Jack was doing, he said, was making us laugh at the frailty of the flesh by telling jokes that ridiculed our pathetic bondage to testes and bowels.

Jack had been given more to stories than to philosophy, but I recalled that once when he had been suffering from an intestinal ailment he had told me that it was a good thing to remember, lest we exalt ourselves too highly, that we are all screwed to the earth through our assholes.

After thirty minutes between the roots, I fell asleep.

The call of a pileated woodpecker split the air like a driven wedge. I had been dreaming about the swamp, and when I opened my eyes on the woods around me I was not quite sure for a moment where I was. Then I heard an insistent flapping and looked up to see the woodpecker. It was hanging nearly upside down on a grapevine not far away, almost as big as a chicken. Even in the subdued light its scarlet crest shone.

Jack had been in my dream. We were hunting together, but somehow he joined a group of men on horseback that included my grandfather and his brothers and cousins. I was surprised that he knew them.

You didn't have to be asleep to see on such a dim morning that the swamp was astir with ghosts. I closed my eyes and a company of generations rode before me, each man dressed in the field clothes of his time, but each with a hunting horn jouncing as he rode. And I saw that my own generation would join them soon, was already beginning to, in fact, for Jack was with them, wearing a red bandanna around his head instead of a tie around his neck, but no different in any other way.

By a campfire someday my son would tell his friends what the Savannah River Swamp had been like when he was a boy; he would tell them about the men in his father's camp, and say that Billy Claypoole was the finest hunter of his time, and that Walter Cabin and Jack Bass and Charlie Creedmore were almost as good. "I wish y'all could have known them," he would say: "they don't make them like that anymore."

Or maybe John would choose not to hunt. Maybe he would find no woods deep enough nor companions worthy enough by virtue of love and knowledge. Or maybe he would just outgrow it, as I so far had not. That would be up to him, but I wondered if he could find an activity that would afford him companionship with such good men as I had known or occasion for establishing a bond with the son that he might have. I doubt that we are sufficiently aware of the extent to which mass-production has damaged the ancient practice of parents passing on to their children the crafts by which they live. What's left for most fathers to teach are baseball and football skills, but I had thought when John came of age that the woodcraft of reading sign and the skills of shooting and dressing game were more important. I was aware of the risks, but he had learned the songfeast, by my own talking and that of the men of the club, the best of all talking, Faulkner calls it, and forever the best of all listening. It had taken, as far as I could tell.

I drew some measure of comfort from that, but not a great deal. The notion that we achieve our only immortality through our children, their names, memories, gestures, and activities, had always struck me as bleak consolation. Rooted to the ground at the base of the oak, I wanted more.

A pileated woodpecker called again. I looked up to see this one winging heavily through the branches. Indian hen, we used to call them, hoping every time that it might be an ivorybill.

My legs had gone to sleep. I needed to get up if I could.

As I began to stir, the deer came, a file of them loping through the grove. Three does and a cowhorn spike. They had not seen me, but the does were suddenly nervous, falling into a stiff-legged jog, jerking their tails. The spike was too smitten with the good fortune of finding these does unattended by a big buck to pay much attention to the world around him, to the man sitting under the tree. I felt a little sorry for it. As I raised my rifle, I realized that it looked exactly like a spike I had killed in that grove two or three years before. Hunh, I thought, maybe they were right— the primitive hunters I had read of who believed that if the hunter slays in the right spirit the animal will live again, to encounter the same man at some point in the future. I hoped so. And shot.

Walking over to the deer, I realized that whether or not it lived again it had died a natural death, for as surely as the wolves and panthers that used to range this riverbottom, I was a predator too, my eyes set like theirs in the front of my head.

I dressed the spike beside a little slough. When I had finished I shoved the offal with my foot into the shallow water. Pigs or possums would dispose of it.

Though it was still early I had no inclination to continue hunting. Maybe in the afternoon, but one deer was enough for this morning. I decided to get Billy's Blazer and take the buck to the cooler. He had parked it at the bridge over Clearwater Stream, more than a mile away. By the time I finished the dragging and the walking and the driving he would be ready to go.

A shot rang out as I was dragging the deer. It was almost too close to course, but my impression was that it had come from the section immediately west of Clearwater Stream. That would be Billy or his guest, though Charlie Creedmore was hunting between them and the river. The shot could have been his.

I left the deer by the road and started walking south. When the bridge came into view, I saw that Charlie's pickup was parked across the road from the Blazer. Directly I saw Charlie stretched out on the ground by the truck. He sat up as I approached. "That you that shot?" he asked.

"An hour or so ago."

He noticed the dried blood on my hands and trousers. "Looks like you got him. You need any help?"

"You can help me load him up. I left him by the road up in L. What about you? Somebody shot not long after I did."

"That must have been Billy or Ed. It wasn't me. What'd you kill?"

"Spike. You see anything?"

"Some tails. You reckon Billy needs help?"

"No. If it was him, he'll field-dress it and put it in the creek, to keep it cool, and go on hunting."

"*Sounds* like an Indian," Charlie said. Then, after a moment, "Here he comes now."

Billy was walking up the road from the west, with that natural, fluid grace that distinguished him from every man I know, and he was holding his rifle like a baton. With his dark green Stetson, his new black moustache, and a three-fifty-seven holstered on his hip he reminded you less of an Indian than of some sepia-toned photograph of a gunfighter or marshal you might have seen in a book about the old west. His face was as blank as a gunfighter's too, but I could tell by the way he was walking—too casually, looking off to either side of the road—that he had game on the ground.

"You ready to do some dragging?" I asked Charlie.

"Hope it's not a pig."

Billy said, "spike," smiling. He had come to the Blazer for a rope. Didn't need any help, thank you, but we were welcome to come along if we liked.

I told Charlie to go ahead. I'd take his truck if that was all right and get my deer and meet them back at the bridge in a little while.

When I returned, Billy and Charlie and Ed were standing on the bridge. Billy's buck looked enough like mine to be its twin.

"Let's get these deer in the water," Billy said. "I want to take y'all somewhere."

We tied ropes around their antlers and lowered them from the bridge into the waist-deep stream, fastening the ropes at the other end to a plank. Seen through the clear water, lying one on top of the other, stiff-legged and slightly bowed, the deer looked unnatural, a little shameful and thrown-away. But the creek would keep them cool till we returned.

I knew it would do no good to ask Billy where we were going, but Charlie didn't.

"Sort of a special place of mine," Billy said. We climbed into the Blazer and headed south.

From the time Billy turned off the main swamp road I was never sure that he followed a marked route. There was no road that I could see. Most of the way it looked to me as though he was weaving through the woods, as trees and fallen logs permitted passage. I didn't see how he could tell where he was going, but presently he stopped at the edge of a dark oxbow.

"That's what they call Bob's Beetree," he said.

I had heard of it, but since it lay south of our designated hunting area I had never been to it. "Looks like you've been here before," I said.

Billy smiled, "Yeah."

Not until I got out of the vehicle did I notice the hill. It rose abruptly on our right from the flat floor of the swamp. Suddenly, things came together. This must be the Indian mound, what they called Rabbit Mount. A team of Harvard archaeologists had done a dig here back in the sixties and published their findings in a monograph.

Billy led us up the side of the mound, through a tangle of cane and smilax. At the top we found one of the pits that the Harvard people had left, a long square hole in the midst of a holly grove; we sat down along its edge with our legs hanging over the sides.

According to the archaeologists, the site was a natural hill rather than a temple or burial mound. They had not been able to determine the earliest period of its occupation, but they found that the most intensive use occurred about 2500 B.C. From that time the hill was occupied sporadically until the coming of de Soto in the sixteenth century.

Billy was kneeling on the floor of the pit, brushing away the loose sandy loam from the wall. Something protruded like a knuckle from the earth. Billy removed it, a discolored bone. Snapping turtle, he said; humerus. Directly the rest of us were making our own little digs, brushing at the walls with our fingers and sifting the soil as it fell. Soon we had collected a pile of antler pieces, various deer bones, more turtle bones, some sherds of pottery, and finally an innocuous fragment that Billy thought might be a piece of human skull. He smiled at me: "You're not the only one with ancestors buried on this plantation." Then he tossed the piece aside.

The wind was picking up, blowing from all quarters, and I was getting chilly. No one said much, preoccupied with his own pictures of what had once occurred there. What I saw was a camp—brown, bare-breasted women scraping stretched deerskin in dappled sunlight, naked children chasing each other among shelters and drying racks, and in the distance hunters coming, a deer suspended from a pole between them. I picked up a piece of antler and tried to envision from its arc the sweep and spread of the whole rack. The stained fragment had once been living tissue, crowning the head of a good-sized buck that had walked the cane thickets of this swamp perhaps when David was king of Israel. It had grown big on the acorns of chestnut oak, and with the coming of cool nights each fall its neck had swollen in rut. Then one day it had fallen, slain by a stone-point arrow, for we had been here too, creating wherever we walked a fear and terror that shaped the life of the animal and made it fleet.

I climbed from the pit and looked out over the swamp. People had been hunting deer in this bottom since the Flood, man and beast engaged in a dance, its gestures, swift or slow, glancing in the sun year after year after year. I looked at Billy and Ed and Charlie: two biologists and a lawyer, dressed in camouflage. An old country man had told me once that a steady diet of wild game would make a man " 'bout half-wild his own se'f." Henry Thoreau had understood that. One of my classes had flinched when Thoreau confesses an impulse to seize and devour a woodchuck raw; someone had said, "Gross!" I had tried to explain that his appetite for wild meat came from living in the woods, but I didn't think they had understood. I wondered what they would say if I walked in like this on Monday, waving a hindquarter of venison.

Charlie said, "Who's got something to eat?"

I said, "Yeah," and we began to stir, stood up and brushed the leaves and dirt from our trousers. As we descended the hill, I noticed that the cloud cover was breaking up, and I wondered, *if the hunter's spirit insures the rebirth of the animal, what does it do for the hunter?*

We gathered at the back of the Blazer and pulled the coolers onto the tailgate. The beer cooler contained one green bottle bobbing without its label in several inches of water, the other a couple of apples, a sandwich somebody had made yesterday and forgotten to eat, a jar of mayonnaise for some reason, and a Tupperware refrigerator dish, Charlie produced a box of Triscuits from somewhere, and that was it—meager fare for hungry men. Billy

opened the Tupperware. It contained something white, creamy with lumps in it. I asked what it was.

"Ed made it," he said. "Try some," and taking a Triscuit scooped a portion and stuck it in my face. I noticed blood stains on his fingernails as I bit the offering from his hand.

"This *is* good. What is it?" I asked and reached for a Triscuit. I wanted another one. But just as I was bringing the food to my mouth I realized that Charlie hadn't tasted it. "Here," I said and offered him the cracker. Billy meanwhile had prepared one for

Ed, and I fixed a second one for myself. Now Billy was reaching into the other cooler. Ed had the Tupperware container, and Charlie was digging into it. "You haven't had one yourself," he said to Billy.

"Will somebody please tell me what we're eating?" I asked. But Billy, who was trying to open the beer against the edge of the tailgate, had taken the cracker from Charlie with his teeth and couldn't answer.

"Seviche," Ed said. "It's a Scandinavian recipe."

"What is it?"

"Fish. You take filleted chunks of raw fish and Vidalia onions and marinate them in lemon juice, or you can use lime, and then mix it with sour cream."

"Raw fish?"

"The lemon juice cooks it. You put it in the fridge for a couple of days."

"What kind of fish do you use?"

"You can use whatever you want. We like bream."

"Jack used to make something like this," Charlie said.

"Is that right?" I said.

"He used them big old bream out of his pond. What he called tittie bream."

We all chuckled. I reached for the bottle and Billy handed it over. I took a long pull and passed it to Charlie, and he in turn handed it on to Ed and fixed a cracker for himself. The crackers and fish went around the circle a few more times, and soon we were scraping up the last of the sour cream, and Charlie finished the beer. By the time we were through, the wind was strong in the tops of the trees and racing across the surface of the oxbow, but the sun had come out and we were all content.

It was too windy to hunt so we lolled about the Blazer telling stories for an hour or so. Billy even tried to fish, but he gave it up after a while, and we went back to the bridge over Clearwater Stream. The deer were stiff and heavy from being in the cold water, and it took all four of us to haul them out.

When we reached the Big Oak, the bandanna was fluttering in the sun, bright red. Billy stopped for a moment and looked at it. Then he tipped the brim of his hat, as though he were adjusting it for comfort, and drove on.

JAMES KILGO is a native of Darlington, South Carolina, and a graduate of Wofford College. He holds M.A. and Ph.D. degrees from Tulane University. He joined the English faculty of the University of Georgia in 1967. He has received the Beaver Award and four Outstanding Honors Professor Awards for excellence in teaching. He and his wife Jane live in Athens, Georgia. They have a son, John, and two daughters, Sarah Jane and Ann. He has contributed essays to *The Sewanee Review* and *The Georgia Review*.